GOD
CALLS YOU
Courageous,
GIRL

JANICE THOMPSON

GOD CALLS YOU
Courageous,
GIRL

180
DEVOTIONS & PRAYERS
for Teens

BARBOUR
PUBLISHING

INTRODUCTION

How do you live a courageous life? The Bible is loaded with verses to inspire you to be braver, bolder, and more confident. But what does this mean exactly?

Simply put, courage is taking your eyes off your own abilities and putting them on God's. When you do that, you're like a modern-day Bible character, ready to change her world for the better!

This little book will equip you to do the things God has called you to do—to be the courageous girl He has called you to be. These 180 devotions will serve as a reminder that, with God's hand in yours, you are capable of great and mighty things!

Think of yourself as a modern-day Esther. You were born for such a time as this, girl! And if God chose to put you here, in the twenty-first century, He will surely give you everything you need to impact the world.

So, what are you waiting for? Look fear in the eye. Remind yourself that it's really God who's in charge. Then step out in faith, ready to do brave and glorious things for Him!

DIFFERENT—AND THAT'S OKAY

My son, do not walk in the way with them;
hold back your foot from their paths.
PROVERBS 1:15 ESV

- -

Have you ever felt different from everyone else? Maybe you don't look like the other girls look. Or maybe you see yourself sticking out like a sore thumb because you're the only Christian in your group.

And yet, despite your differences, God has called you to be a world changer. In your friend group. At your school. Even at church with the girls who claim to be one thing but are different when no one is looking.

There's an amazing story in the Bible about a young woman named Esther. She was a Jewish girl in a culture that looked down on Jews. Somehow—miraculously—she was chosen by the king to be his wife. A Jewish queen? How could she possibly fill that role when so many people looked down on the Jews?

God moved miraculously through Esther. In fact, He ended up saving her people because of her bravery. He's able to do amazing things when people step up with courage and make themselves available to Him.

You're no different. God wants to use you, just as He used Esther. Place your trust in Him. Take a deep breath. Then step out! Miracles will happen!

I'm willing to be different if it means I will please You, Lord! Amen.

WHEN YOU DON'T FIT IN

Do not be conformed to this world, but be transformed by the renewal of your mind, that by testing you may discern what is the will of God, what is good and acceptable and perfect.

ROMANS 12:2 ESV

Knowing that your faith sets you apart from modern culture can be scary. In many ways, you're like Esther, surrounded on every side by people with different beliefs and customs. So what do you do? Does God want you to blend in, or does He have another plan in mind for you?

Esther never changed who she was so that she could blend in. She owned her differences and used them to her advantage. Don't hide your beliefs so that you can fit in, girl. Things won't end well.

Look at today's verse. Romans 12:2 says that you're not supposed to conform to this world. What does it mean to conform? It's just like putty or Play-Doh being squeezed into a mold. The putty takes on the shape of the mold.

The only mold you need to fit yourself into is the mold of Jesus. It will take courage not to squeeze yourself into the mold your friends and acquaintances are in. But when you start acting, talking, and behaving like them? Well, that never ends well.

Be brave. Don't conform!

I only want to look and act like You, Jesus,
but I'll need Your help to pull this off! Amen.

SET APART

*"You have been set apart as holy to the LORD your
God, and he has chosen you from all the nations of
the earth to be his own special treasure."*
DEUTERONOMY 14:2 NLT

Imagine you're shopping with your mom at the grocery store. She buys a ton of fruit. And when she pulls out a bushel of peaches, your mouth waters. They're your favorite. You reach for one, but she gives you a stern look.

"No," she says. "I'm setting those aside for something special. I'm going to make a peach cobbler for tonight's dessert."

Well, that changes everything! You don't mind waiting now, because something better is coming!

In some ways, you are like that bushel of peaches. You have been set apart by God for great things. He has amazing plans for you. So don't be in a rush to get to all the good stuff now. It takes courage to wait, to be different. And remember, peaches take time to ripen. But when the time is right, they are transformed into the most delicious dessert ever!

*I get it, Jesus! You've set me apart to be different
from the world. I'll be patient and courageous while
I wait for the good stuff to come! Amen.*

COME OUT

"Therefore, come out from among unbelievers, and separate yourselves from them, says the Lord. Don't touch their filthy things, and I will welcome you."
2 Corinthians 6:17 NLT

Sometimes it takes more courage not to do something, doesn't it? Say you're with a group of friends and they're hot and heavy in a gossip session about a girl they don't like. You know this girl, and she's never done anything to hurt you. But you find yourself saying awful things about her, just to fit in.

Or maybe one of your friends is bragging about her latest escapades with her boyfriend and you get drawn into the conversation. Before long, you're giggling and laughing and congratulating her about what she's done, as if it's all good and right.

Only, it's not. And you know it.

It takes courage to stop yourself from saying the things gossips want you to say. God knew this, and that's why His Word says that we are to "come out from among unbelievers, and separate [ourselves] from them." Be kind, but remember—the people you should be hanging close with are the ones who won't try to lead you down the wrong path.

I want to be set apart, Jesus, but I know it's going to take courage. Help me with the things I'm not supposed to be doing. I don't want to break Your heart. Amen.

BE HOLY AS GOD IS HOLY

So then, have your minds ready for action. Keep alert and set your hope completely on the blessing which will be given you when Jesus Christ is revealed. Be obedient to God, and do not allow your lives to be shaped by those desires you had when you were still ignorant. Instead, be holy in all that you do, just as God who called you is holy. The scripture says, "Be holy because I am holy."
1 PETER 1:13–16 GNT

Some people think that being "holy" means you follow a list of dos and don'ts so it looks like you're a good girl. The problem with that approach is obvious: you can only keep it up for so long. Faking is hard work.

God doesn't want your holiness to be faked. He's longing for clean hands and a pure heart from you. That means even when you're around your friends.

This modern-day culture will try to rob you of your innocence. Don't let it! It will take courage to say no to all the things society wants you to say yes to, but you can do it. Be like Esther. Be courageous even when everyone around you believes differently than you.

Your holiness is pleasing to God. Isn't that a thousand times better than fitting in with your friends?

I want to please You, Jesus. No more faking it. I want to be holy. . . for real! But I will definitely need Your help with this. Amen.

BLAMELESS AND INNOCENT

That you may be blameless and innocent, children of God without blemish in the midst of a crooked and twisted generation, among whom you shine as lights in the world.
PHILIPPIANS 2:15 ESV

Two thousand years ago—before there were planes, trains, or automobiles, before there were cell phones, computers, or the internet—God instructed His people to be blameless and innocent in the very middle of a crooked and twisted generation.

It's kind of crazy to think that people have always been twisted, even before social media! (Let's face it—people can get kind of nuts when they're posting pictures and comments online or by text.)

God always knew that the world was broken. It was then, and it is now. We could argue about whether the world is better or worse than it was two thousand years ago, but the truth is it's still twisted and perverted.

And somehow, in the middle of it all, God wants you to remain blameless and innocent. Like Esther, you have to courageously take a stand. Your faith will be honored and rewarded. What joy it brings to God's heart when His daughters remain pure!

Lord, with Your help, I can do it. I'll stand strong, and I won't bow down to this twisted generation! Amen.

HE HAS CALLED YOU HIS OWN

Remember that the LORD has chosen the righteous for
his own, and he hears me when I call to him.
PSALM 4:3 GNT

Esther was chosen to be set apart from the others around her. She was the king's intended, his bride. Living in a palace must have seemed really strange. She was just a simple girl, after all! But God had big things for her to accomplish there.

God has big things for you too. That's why He has set you apart from the others who live differently. The goal was never for you to fit in; it was always for you to stand up and stand out for Him.

Different is good. When God looks at the crowd of humanity, may He point to you and say, "See that girl right there? She gets it! She cares more about Me than she does about fitting in."

He set you apart. And because you're so special to Him, He sticks closer than any friend. He's right there, ready to answer when you call.

I get it, Jesus. You don't want me to spend so much time trying to figure out how or where I fit in. You simply want me to love You passionately and to stay focused on my relationship with You. You'll work everything else out to Your glory! Amen.

SETTLE THE ISSUE IN YOUR HEART

*Do not let my heart be drawn to what is evil so that I
take part in wicked deeds along with those who are
evildoers; do not let me eat their delicacies.*
PSALM 141:4 NIV

You're confronted on every side—when you turn on the TV, when you go to the movies, when you open a magazine, when you hang out with your friends. They all seem to be delivering one solid message: that you need to embrace what the Bible clearly says is evil and call it good.

Here's the thing: God's Word never changes. Never ever. . .in the history of, well, ever. The Word of God is just as real and honest today as it was when the words were written. If the Bible calls something bad, it's bad. Even if you spend twenty-four hours a day saying it's good, that won't change the truth of God's Word.

You really can turn your heart from evil if you settle the issue in your mind that it's truly breaking God's heart. Your goal, as His daughter, is to bring joy to His heart, not sadness. So make up your mind, girl! Turn from the things that cause pain to your heavenly Father, even if it means being courageous in front of your friends.

*I don't want to break Your heart, Lord. I know what
Your Word says, and I know it's all true and right. Help
me to stick to the Bible even when it's hard. Amen.*

LET YOUR LIGHT SHINE

Do not love this world nor the things it offers you, for when you love the world, you do not have the love of the Father in you.
1 JOHN 2:15 NLT

If you break this verse down, it can be quite painful! When you love the world (and the things it offers), you don't have the love of the Father in you. Ouch!

You're tempted to try to love the world and love Jesus at the same time. But He never meant for this to happen. Sure, you must live in the world. And yes, you must love those who surround you. But to delight in the things they delight in? To call "good" the things they call good? God never meant for you to live that way.

Your goal, as a believer in this culture, is to shine like a bright light. In a loving way. In a humble way. In a tender and gentle way. But guard your heart! If you feel that you're starting to tip in the direction of worldly beliefs and goals, it's time to reassess! Back away from the fire and draw close to Jesus once again. Ask Him to refill you and give you the tools you need to go on living in this crazy culture while remaining pure and holy. He will help you!

*I won't fall in love with the world, Jesus!
My heart is Yours completely! Amen.*

THE WORLD'S BELIEF SYSTEM

"I do not ask that you take them out of the world, but that you keep them from the evil one. They are not of the world, just as I am not of the world. Sanctify them in the truth; your word is truth. As you sent me into the world, so I have sent them into the world."
JOHN 17:15–18 ESV

This world is a crazy place! It seems kind of inside out and upside down at times. The way people live today doesn't really match up with how the Bible says they should.

And yet God has placed you here on this earth to live out your life and to make a difference.

You are here on purpose. God is not going to open a magic window and sweep us away. But while we're here, we do have an obligation to Him to stay away from the enemy and his plans for us. (Did you realize the enemy has plans for your life, just like God does? It's true.)

You might wonder, *How do I do that? How can I live in the world but not get swept up in its belief system?* The answer is found in today's verse: "Sanctify them in the truth; your word is truth." You must cling to the Bible and the teachings you find inside. They won't match culture, that's for sure. But if there's ever a discrepancy between biblical truth and culture, it's important that you choose the Bible—every single time.

*I'll follow Your plans, Lord, not the enemy's.
And I'll stick with the Bible. I know it's filled
with truth that will save me from disaster. Amen.*

EVEN THE BIG STUFF

*For I, the L*ORD *your God, hold your right hand; it is I who say to you, "Fear not, I am the one who helps you."*
ISAIAH 41:13 ESV

• •

Sometimes God calls us to do big things. Really big things. Our knees shake, our hands tremble, and we spend days and nights convincing ourselves we can't possibly do it.

Only, of course, we usually have no choice. So we plow ahead, terror in our hearts, and do the very best we can.

Have you been through an experience like that? Maybe you had to make a presentation in front of a large group or sing a solo in front of the whole school. Maybe you had to apologize to someone you'd hurt and the apology terrified you. Perhaps you had to confess something to your parents that you had done, something really awful.

There will always be uncomfortable, scary situations we're asked to face. But, like Esther, it's better to go ahead and face them. Remember, if you do the right thing, God will walk with you every step of the way. And if you don't? If you choose not to obey? Well, let's just say things could get even scarier!

Lord, I want to obey even when I'm terrified! I know You'll go with me and help me. I will do what needs to be done. Give me courage, I pray. Amen.

EXPOSURE

Have nothing to do with the fruitless deeds
of darkness, but rather expose them.
EPHESIANS 5:11 NIV

Why do you suppose God says we should expose deeds of darkness?
Is He asking you to rat out all your friends who do the wrong things?

Think about it this way: As a believer, you're a light in a dark world.
The role of light is to expose things hidden in the shadows. So, whether
you mean to do it or not, you're already exposing evil deeds of darkness,
every time you enter a place.

Keep shining that light. When you do, the darkness will flee. But
remember, God also instructs you to "have nothing to do with the fruitless deeds of darkness." So, while you might be surrounded by shadows,
you're not supposed to participate in the evil that goes on there.

It's possible to be in this world but not swallowed up by it. Shine
your light, but stay pure, girl. You will make an amazing difference
when you do.

Thank You for shining Your light through me, Jesus.
I want to make a difference in this world. Help me to
stay away from the evil deeds of darkness that often
surround me so that I can remain strong in You. Amen.

BECAUSE HE LOVES YOU

For God gave us a spirit not of fear but
of power and love and self-control.
2 TIMOTHY 1:7 ESV

Sometimes it feels like fear is an uncontrollable thing, but God gave you power over it. This doesn't mean you won't occasionally be struck with feelings of fear, but remember: they're just feelings; they have no power over you.

Surely Esther felt strong feelings of fear as she left her homeland and her people to travel to a strange new place. But she made up her mind to not let fear control her.

How did she do that? No doubt she followed the formula found in today's verse: instead of dwelling on the spirit of fear, she gave over her thoughts to God's power, His love, and Spirit-driven self-control.

Here's the truth: When you really truly put your trust in your Creator, you gain His power to overcome. When you understand His great love for you, you learn to trust Him even in the scariest moments. God gives you the self-control you need to not give in to fear.

In other words, fall in love with Jesus and He equips you with courage, power, and good thoughts.

I trust You, Jesus! I know You love me,
and this helps me overcome every fear! Amen.

JUST DO IT

David also said to Solomon his son, "Be strong and courageous,
and do the work. Do not be afraid or discouraged, for the Lord
God, my God, is with you. He will not fail you or forsake you until
all the work for the service of the temple of the Lord is finished."
1 Chronicles 28:20 niv

No doubt you've seen the "Just do it" logo. Sometimes you need that added encouragement to move forward when you don't feel like it.

When you're facing a challenge of supernatural proportions, God says, "Just do it!"

When you're afraid and feel frozen in place, He whispers, "You can, girl."

Just as David said to his son Solomon, "Be strong and courageous, and do the work," God says, "Be brave and do it even if you feel like you can't."

When you receive those words of encouragement, you're suddenly infused with zeal that you didn't have before. So don't be afraid. Don't get discouraged. The Creator of the universe is whispering in your ear even now, "You've got this, girl. Just do it."

Jesus, I'm so scared sometimes. This world is a crazy place!
But when I hear You giving me those little nudges, I suddenly
feel braver than before. Thank You, Lord! Amen.

HE'S NOT LIKE THE WORLD

"Peace I leave with you; my peace I give you.
I do not give to you as the world gives. Do not let
your hearts be troubled and do not be afraid."
JOHN 14:27 NIV

Check out this amazing verse from the Gospel of John. Jesus promises to give you peace—whether you're walking through a storm, going through a health crisis, or facing opposition from people you thought were your friends.

Not only will God give you the courage to get through rough seasons, but He will also give you supernatural peace in place of fear. Maybe you hear the word *peace* and you think of a day at the beach or a quiet getaway in the woods far from people and noise.

Read the rest of the verse. God doesn't give the same kind of peace the world gives. It's not found in spas or a day at the beach (though those things are fun and good). The kind of peace He gives goes w-a-a-a-y beyond all that. It's not temporary. It's truly supernatural! So don't be afraid. Don't be troubled. You really can trust Him even in the toughest seasons.

Jesus, thank You! There are days when I need that kind of peace.
I'm so glad You love me enough to give it to me! Amen.

BASIC TRAINING

*Finally, build up your strength in union with
the Lord and by means of his mighty power.*
Ephesians 6:10 gnt

• •

Have you ever seen a movie or video clip of someone who has recently joined the military? All new recruits must go through what is called basic training. During this training, a lot of physical exercises take place. They're meant to toughen the body.

Recruits are toughened in other ways too. Sometimes their supervisors are deliberately mean to them. They get in their faces and yell. They make things harder than they need to be.

Why? . . . Perhaps it's so that the young recruit can learn early on how to face opposition and not panic. It's better to learn this skill during basic training than on the battleground! The recruit is toughening up, on the outside and the inside too. That way, when the real battle comes, the new soldier will have everything needed to stand strong.

God wants you to be just as tough. Today's verse says you should be strong in the Lord and in His mighty power. You'll never be tough enough on your own. The challenges you face are strengthening you to be everything you need to be!

*I get it, Lord. The only way I'm going to be able to
stand strong is if I submit to the process. I'll go through
spiritual basic training. I'll give my heart, mind, body,
and soul to You so that You can use me. Amen.*

THE LAST LEAF

Look to the LORD and his strength; seek his face always.
1 CHRONICLES 16:11 NIV

There's a great short story by O. Henry called "The Last Leaf." In it a dying woman watches out the window every day as leaves fall from a tree near the property wall. She tells herself that she will hang on until the last leaf falls. Remarkably, the last leaf never falls. It holds on for dear life. And the young woman decides to keep fighting for her life.

We learn at the end of the story that an artist painted the leaf on the wall to give the illusion of being real. He gave his life to accomplish this. But it worked—the woman didn't give up.

You shouldn't give up either. There will be many times you feel like it, for sure. You'll want to quit because you feel overwhelmed. But Jesus is the leaf on the wall. He's the rock-solid one giving you strength even when you're not feeling it. So be like the girl in the story. Keep your focus on Him, not yourself. Even when you think you can't. . .He can.

Thank You for giving me strength, Lord! I'll do my best to keep my eyes on You and to lean on Your strength. Amen.

WHILE YOU'RE WAITING

Be strong, and let your heart take courage,
all you who wait for the LORD!
PSALM 31:24 ESV

Have you ever been late to an appointment or school event? Maybe your choir director said, "Be at the school by six thirty to warm up for the concert." Only Mom never showed up from work to take you there, so you didn't get to the school until almost seven.

Those incidents can be nerve-racking, especially if you're the type of person to fret over time. It's not easy to wait, especially when you know something should be happening.

The same is true in your faith walk. Maybe you're waiting on God to answer a prayer. A big one. You wait and wait, but He never seems to show up. You feel like you're going to be late to the proverbial concert.

And then, in His own special way, God sweeps in and performs a miracle. He answers your prayers in ways even better than you could have anticipated.

While you're waiting (and you will), be strong. Have courage. Trust in God's plan for you no matter how long it takes.

I'll keep waiting, Jesus. I won't give up or grow weary while
I'm waiting on You to do what I know You'll do. Amen.

WRITE IT DOWN

"Put it in writing, because it is not yet time for it to come true. But the time is coming quickly, and what I show you will come true. It may seem slow in coming, but wait for it; it will certainly take place, and it will not be delayed."
<small>HABAKKUK 2:3 GNT</small>

- -

Sometimes you stand in faith, believing that God will perform a miracle for you. Time goes by and you forget. That's why it's good to write things down.

Instead of just "hoping" for something, commit it to paper. Then pray over that paper. Bring it up in prayer often.

You'll probably grow weak in your faith over time if you don't refer back to what you've written down, so put it in a place where you'll have to see it every day: Tape it to your bathroom window. Use a magnet to fasten it to the refrigerator. Place it on the bedside table. Then, as your faith disappears, you'll be forced to remind yourself of what you're standing in faith for.

And don't worry about the time lapse. God never said He was going to move instantly, after all. He has a very specific timetable, one we don't understand. Just keep on believing, keep on standing, and keep on proclaiming His goodness while you're waiting.

The time is coming, Lord. I know it is. So I won't give up while I'm waiting. I'll remind myself daily that You've never let me down yet and You never will. Amen.

WHAT ARE YOU BELIEVING FOR?

Be patient, therefore, brothers, until the coming of the Lord. See how the farmer waits for the precious fruit of the earth, being patient about it, until it receives the early and the late rains.

JAMES 5:7 ESV

Can you imagine being a farmer? You plant your seeds, and then you wait. You water the ground and hope you'll eventually see signs of life. Finally! A little green sprout springs up! So you keep watering. You keep tending. You keep hoping.

A farmer must believe that his seeds will produce real food. The same is true with your faith. Even when your courage seems to be disappearing, you must keep believing that God hasn't left you and He never will.

What are you believing God for today? Don't give up, girl. Be patient, just as the farmer is patient. It takes time for seeds to sprout and for the season of harvest to come. In the meantime, water your faith with prayer and by reading the Bible. Those verses about faith will keep you going until that miracle comes.

I will be courageous while I wait, Lord. I don't always feel like it, especially when my prayers seem to be unanswered. But, like the farmer waits for tiny sprouts to show up, I'll keep waiting too. Amen.

MY ANSWER IS YES

As Jesus walked beside the Sea of Galilee, he saw Simon and his brother Andrew casting a net into the lake, for they were fishermen. "Come, follow me," Jesus said, "and I will send you out to fish for people." At once they left their nets and followed him.
MARK 1:16–18 NIV

• •

Imagine you're invited to a party. You check your calendar and see that you've already got a big family event on that same day. In other words, you're unavailable. You're sad, but what can you do? You have a prior commitment, after all, and you don't want to let your family down.

Jesus wants you to make yourself available to Him 24/7, 365 days a year. That might sound overwhelming, but part of being a believer means going where He calls you to go and doing what He calls you to do.

Esther understood this. She was asked to do a hard thing. No doubt everything inside of her wanted to say, "Nope, sorry! I'm not available for that!" But she didn't argue. She simply stepped out in faith and did the hard thing. And because she did, an entire people group was saved. Wow!

Availability is a gift you give to God. And in return He uses you to do amazing things!

I will make myself available to You, Jesus! I want to do great things for You. Amen.

AVAILABLE. . .WITHOUT ATTITUDE

So then each of us will give an account of himself to God.
ROMANS 14:12 ESV

Mom is asking you to babysit your younger siblings. . .again. She has to work, and someone has to be in charge.

So you do it, but your heart isn't in it. You're grumpy with the kids and irritated at your mom, and you basically ruin everyone's day. Technically, you've made yourself available, but in your heart you're rebelling every step of the way.

Here's the thing: When you say yes to the things God asks you to do, He wants that yes to be an attitude-free one. That means no half-hearted or grumpy efforts. When you say yes with your whole heart, you dive right in, making the experience as pleasant for everyone as possible.

These types of yeses please the heart of God. And guess what? You end up having a better day too! So offer up your availability—without attitude!

*(Deep sigh!) Okay, okay, I get it, Lord. You want my yes,
but You want it with a happy heart. Sometimes I make things
harder than they need to be because I get frustrated. Help
me to make myself available with a joyful heart. Amen.*

A GREAT PRESENTATION

*So then, my friends, because of God's great mercy to us
I appeal to you: Offer yourselves as a living sacrifice
to God, dedicated to his service and pleasing to him.
This is the true worship that you should offer.*

ROMANS 12:1 GNT

- -

Have you ever had to give a presentation in school? Maybe you worked for weeks on a replica of the Eiffel Tower, then stood in front of your French class to share all that you learned about it.

When you "present" that replica to your teacher and class, you're (hopefully) giving them your best work. It's embarrassing to present shoddy work, after all. If your version of the Eiffel Tower crumbled and fell at your feet, how awkward would that be?

God wants you to present yourself, much as you would present a school project, but He asks for even more than a great presentation. He wants you to sacrifice yourself for the sake of the kingdom. He asks you to do hard things—to stand for what is right even if everyone else in the room is cratering to peer pressure.

You can do it. Even if you feel like you can't. Offer yourself to Him—fully, wholly—heart, mind, and soul. God will then use you to reach others and change the world.

*Jesus, I present myself to You. I know the journey won't always
be easy, but I am willing to give You my very best. Amen.*

IF NOT YOU, THEN WHO?

*And I heard the voice of the Lord saying, "Whom shall I send,
and who will go for us?" Then I said, "Here I am! Send me."*
ISAIAH 6:8 ESV

It's true that God asks you to go outside of your comfort zone at times.
He might ask you to have a hard conversation with a friend about some
of her lifestyle choices. Or maybe He'll ask you to take a stand for something
in the Bible even if most of your friends disagree.

This life isn't always easy. But think about it this way: If you refuse
to make yourself available and say, "God, please pick someone else!"
then what happens if no one else ever steps up? Will your friend ever
hear the truth? Will change ever come in the hearts and lives of those
you love? Your availability could change everything for someone who is
teetering on the ledge between the truth and a lie. She could step into
the truth if you just have the courage to speak it.

Hard question: If not you, then who?

Don't make God have to work overtime looking for someone else
to do the things you're too scared to do. Step out of your comfort zone.
Say, "Here I am, Lord. Use me!"

*Here I am, Lord. Use me! I mean that even when it's
hard to speak up. Even when everyone else disagrees
with me. I'm still here, ready to make myself available
to You. Make me brave. Here I am! Amen.*

LISTEN UP!

*"Incline your ear, and come to me; hear, that your
soul may live; and I will make with you an everlasting
covenant, my steadfast, sure love for David."*
ISAIAH 55:3 ESV

Do you ever tune out people? Maybe you're in history class and the teacher is giving a lecture about ancient Mesopotamia. You stare at the clock, and then your thoughts shift to your plans for this coming weekend. You're going to the beach with your friend's family. It's going to be so much fun.

In the middle of your daydream about the warm sun, the cool waves, and the smell of coconut suntan lotion, the teacher calls your name. Actually, she calls your name three times, but you don't hear it the first two because you're zoned out. Only when the kid next to you jabs you to get your attention do you wake up.

We all zone out, but when it comes to spending time with God, He wants your full attention. "Incline" your ear to Him. That means *Listen up, kid!* Why? So that your soul can live! Don't tune out God. It's only fair, after all! He's never tuned you out, not even once! So give Him your full, undivided attention.

*You give me so much, Jesus. It's only fair that I give You all of me
in return. I'll do a better job of tuning in from now on. I don't
want to miss a thing on this adventure with You! Amen.*

HERE I AM

When the LORD saw that he turned aside to see, God called to him out of the bush, "Moses, Moses!" And he said, "Here I am."
EXODUS 3:4 ESV

It takes a lot of courage to step out into your calling, especially when you see yourself as flawed. Maybe you look in the mirror and all you see are the blemishes. The problem spots. You question so many things about yourself—your abilities, your talents, your usability.

Here's the thing: God called Moses—a man who stuttered and had little confidence in himself—to do a huge task.

The same thing happened with Esther—and a lot of other Bible characters too. And you're just like them. You know your own shortcomings better than anyone, after all. So you have doubts. You wish God would pick someone else. You say, "Hey, there's another girl in my Bible study group who would be so much better at this, Lord."

But He has picked you. And He wants your response to be "Yes, Lord! I'll go. Here I am. Send me."

Are you ready to lay down your insecurities and step into your purpose? Today's the day! Don't wait a moment longer.

Here I am, Lord! No hiding. No excuses. I'm ready for whatever You're calling me to do! Amen.

A HOLY CALLING

[God] saved us and called us to a holy calling, not because
of our works but because of his own purpose and grace,
which he gave us in Christ Jesus before the ages began.
2 TIMOTHY 1:9 ESV

Did you know that there are certain things God has called you to do with your life? He has plans for you that no one else could accomplish. You might hear that and say, "Are You sure, Lord?"

He's sure. He has given you a holy calling. And here's the thing: Because it's a holy (heavenly) calling, the outcome is up to God, not you. So you can take a deep breath, girl. Rest easy. It's not because of your good works that He has called you; it's because of His own purpose (His plans) and His grace.

How does grace work? Well, it takes all your shortcomings, all your flaws, and overlooks them. When God looks at you, He doesn't see a flawed girl. He sees a girl who has given herself to Him, usable and ready for service!

I'm so grateful for this holy calling You have placed on my life, Lord!
I want to do my best to live it out, but I'll need Your help. Amen.

AFTER ALL THESE THINGS

*After these things God tested Abraham and said
to him, "Abraham!" And he said, "Here I am."*
GENESIS 22:1 ESV

- -

"After these things."

Read those words again. "After these things God tested Abraham."

Maybe you can relate. Maybe you've been through a rough season. To your way of thinking, this is the absolute worst time God could possibly ask anything more of you.

And yet He does. In the middle of your overwhelmed moment, He calls out to you with a big task, one that seems impossible to you.

And you panic. You say, "Um, no. No thanks. Not now. I'm still recovering from the hard season I just walked through."

Oh, but listen, sweet girl: That hard season has shaped and defined you and has given you the courage to face the situations in front of you. Without it, you wouldn't have the knowledge or the inner strength to tackle what's coming around the bend. So go ahead and say, "Here I am, Lord!" because God is going to give you everything you need to keep going.

*Sometimes I hardly catch my breath before the next
big task comes along. But I'll say yes to You, Lord. I
trust You even when I'm overwhelmed. Amen.*

PICK ME, LORD!

Then the LORD called Samuel, and he said, "Here I am!"
1 SAMUEL 3:4 ESV

"Here I am!"

Are you noticing a theme in the last few Bible verses? There are several accounts in the Bible where God called someone to do something big. Repeatedly, the person's answer was "Here I am!"

When you have a "Here I am, send me!" response in your heart to whatever God calls you to do, guess what? He calls on you more often! It's like that kid in class who raises his hand to answer the math problem. The more you raise your hand, the more often you get called on.

Moses raised his hand. Samuel raised his hand. Isaiah raised his hand. Esther raised her hand.

They all said, "Pick me, Lord!" And He did. Their stories aren't fiction. They're very real accounts of people who said yes and then accomplished remarkable things. Be the one who raises your hand to say yes to whatever God asks of you. When you live a "Yes, Lord!" life, you will do tremendous things for Him. (And who knows! Maybe one day people will be writing stories about all the lives that were changed because of your yes!)

Today and every day I say yes to You, Lord! Thanks for giving me the courage to raise my hand! Amen.

BEFORE THE FOUNDATION
OF THE WORLD

Even as he chose us in him before the foundation of the
world, that we should be holy and blameless before him.
In love he predestined us for adoption to himself as sons
through Jesus Christ, according to the purpose of his will.
EPHESIANS 1:4–5 ESV

There's an amazing message in today's scripture, one that could absolutely change your life if you let it.

God chose you before the foundation of the world. Before there were stars. Or grass. Or giraffes. Before rivers flowed into the seas. Before mountain peaks rose in majesty. Before bluebirds sang their first song.

God chose you—yes, you—as His child. He knew you would be adopted into His family even before you were born. (That's crazy to think about, right?)

And because you're part of the family, He also knew that you would learn to live a life worthy of being His child. A holy life. A blameless life. A life of purity and grace.

That's what it means to be His adopted child. He gives you everything you need. . .and more!

Wow, Jesus! It's crazy to think You knew me before
the world was even formed! Thank You for investing
in me all these many, many years! Amen.

A BEAUTIFUL QUEEN

Now the king was attracted to Esther more than to any of the other women, and she won his favor and approval more than any of the other virgins. So he set a royal crown on her head and made her queen instead of Vashti. And the king gave a great banquet, Esther's banquet, for all his nobles and officials. He proclaimed a holiday throughout the provinces and distributed gifts with royal liberality.
ESTHER 2:17–18 NIV

When Esther married the king, she became royalty. She went from being an ordinary girl to being a queen! A queen looks different. Acts differently. A queen speaks differently too!

When you gave your heart to Jesus, just like Esther, you became royalty! (It's true!) Jesus is the King of kings and Lord of lords. Your heart is forever entwined with His, and this means you are a princess.

Being a princess has its privileges. You have access to the King! You live your life with a different purpose. You know without a doubt that the King will take care of you no matter what.

And, best of all, you know how truly loved you are. You belong to Him, after all!

Thank You for making me part of the royal family, Jesus! I will live as a royal daughter should. Amen.

A READY HEART

All glorious is the princess in her chamber, with robes interwoven with gold. In many-colored robes she is led to the king, with her virgin companions following behind her. With joy and gladness they are led along as they enter the palace of the king.

PSALM 45:13–15 ESV

"In many-colored robes she is led to the king." What comes to mind as you read those words? Can you almost envision the incoming queen getting dressed up—putting on jewelry, having her hair fixed—in preparation to see the king?

In much the same way, you are to prepare yourself to spend time with Jesus. Get your heart ready. Push aside anything that might keep you from spending quality time together. With joy and gladness, come to Him each day. Sing a worship song. Pray. Read His Word. Tell Him how much you love Him. Let Him show you how much He loves you.

These intimate times with Him will embolden you and give you the courage and strength you need to go out and face your day, so don't skip that alone time. How precious for the princess to have time in the inner courts with the King of kings!

I'm ready to meet with You, Jesus! Here I come, with worship on my lips and joy in my heart! Amen.

NOT FEELING IT

*"And you have made them a kingdom and priests
to our God, and they shall reign on the earth."*
REVELATION 5:10 ESV

Maybe you're just not feeling it some days. You hear the words "you're a daughter of the Most High God," and you flinch. You certainly don't feel like a princess. You feel like a pauper from the far side of the kingdom with no aspirations of royalty whatsoever.

Here's the thing: how you feel doesn't define who you are. And that is proven in today's verse. Jesus made us "a kingdom and priests to our God." That means He decided what—and who—you would be. He hand selected you to serve Him, to love Him, and to live the life of a daughter of the King.

Yes, you'll still have days when you're not feeling it. But even then—*especially* then—you can lean on this verse. You were made to reign on the earth, girl! So straighten that crown and get busy!

*I'll admit, I don't always feel very princess-like, Lord.
Some days I'd rather not rule and reign, thank You very much!
On those days, please help me to remember that I'm supposed
to represent You while I'm here on this earth. I want to do
my best so that others will come to know You too. Amen.*

YOU ARE HIS OWN

But you are a chosen race, a royal priesthood,
a holy nation, a people for his own possession,
that you may proclaim the excellencies of him who
called you out of darkness into his marvelous light.
1 PETER 2:9 ESV

Remember how you used to love to play with dolls when you were a little girl? Maybe you collected a bunch of them. Or maybe you just had one that you kept with you much of the time because she was so special to you.

If someone asked, "Whose doll is that?" you would answer, "She's mine! I own her!" (And heaven help anyone who tried to take her from you, especially a younger sibling!)

Think about that doll in light of today's verse. It says that you belong to God, just like that doll belonged to you. You are "a people for his own possession." He doesn't own you as if He were a slave owner; He owns you as a loving Father! And just as you felt possession and ownership over that precious baby doll, He feels that and a million times more for you.

Knowing you were chosen to be loved by your heavenly Father should make you courageous! You're a child of the King, meant to do great and mighty things!

I love that You love me, Jesus! I belong to You! Help me show
that same kind of love to everyone around me. Amen.

YOU ARE HIS CROWN

*Then you will be a beautiful crown in the hand of
the LORD, a royal crown in the hand of your God.*
ISAIAH 62:3 GW

When you read today's verse, what image comes to mind? Do you see
God holding a literal crown in His hand? Do you see bright, sparkling
jewels, radiating beauty and light?

You are the crown in His hand, sweet girl. *You.* Even on rough days,
when you're not feeling it. (Hey, we all have those days!)

Even then, you're a beautiful crown in His hand. As Your Father, He
wants to show you off and let your gifts soar. That's what happens to
kids who belong to the King. They get preferential treatment. (You know
it's true! Every prince or princess was pampered, after all!)

Do you see yourself as a beautiful daughter of the King? Then do
your best to radiate the heavenly beauty He has placed inside you!

Today, pause to thank Him for making you to be a brilliant crown
on display for all the world to see.

*I want to reflect You well, Lord! May I shine brightly
for You in this dark and messed-up world. Amen.*

SEATED ON HIS THRONE

*"And he will reign over Israel forever;
his Kingdom will never end!"*
LUKE 1:33 NLT

Every king who has ever reigned has only done so for a set period of time, from the moment he took the throne to the moment he died. The same is true with queens. Queen Elizabeth II, head of the British monarchy, reigned until her death in 2022.

Now think about God's reign. It started before the foundation of the world and will go on into eternity. He will never give up the throne. Satan has been trying (since the beginning, really) to knock God off that throne, but the Almighty is not going anywhere.

And neither are you! You are supposed to rule and reign alongside the Lord. And now that you've accepted Christ into your heart (you have, haven't you?), then you're promised eternity with Him. That means you'll be part of this royal family forever!

*Lord, thank You for adopting me into Your royal family!
It's so exciting to realize that You have called me to
live with royal authority in this life. And I'm so blessed
and humbled that I get to spend eternity with You
and all the others in Your special family. Amen.*

MUCH IS REQUIRED

*"Much is required from those to whom much
is given, for their responsibility is greater."*
Luke 12:48 tlb

. . . .

The person who is given much has a higher level of responsibility. What a fascinating concept! Would you say that you have been given much? Do you have a home to live in? Shoes to wear? Food on the table? If so, then you have more than most people in the world.

So what does this mean? If you've been blessed, you need to be a blessing to others. And because you're a daughter of the Most High King, you're doubly blessed! So you must share the good news with as much joy as you would share a cup of water with a thirsty person on the side of the road.

Maybe you've heard the expression "Give it away." Give joy. Give hope. Give the gospel. Give food. Give clothes. Give generously. Because you're so incredibly blessed, go out and bless those you meet. This will take courage, but God will show you creative ways to be generous.

*I want to pour myself out, Lord. I want to bless others
the way You've blessed me. I realize this will require
courage, but as a daughter of the King, I have the best
possible Father watching over me. Thank You for showing
me how to bless others courageously. Amen.*

FROM THE INSIDE OUT

Instead, your beauty should consist of your true inner self, the ageless beauty of a gentle and quiet spirit, which is of the greatest value in God's sight.

1 PETER 3:4 GNT

. . . .

You want to look your best, and you try to keep up with the latest fashion and beauty trends, but sometimes it all feels a little, well, silly. Fashion reels on social media are fun to look at, but when it comes to looking like those women, who can possibly compare?

It takes courage not to focus too much on your external beauty, but the Bible says that a girl's beauty should be internal. There's something special about a woman who is beautiful from the inside out. The Word of God calls this "ageless" beauty. And that's really true! An eighty-year-old woman can be just as gorgeous as a twenty-year-old fashion model.

To be beautiful from the inside out, you have to have a gentle spirit and treat others kindly. There's no mascara or lip gloss that will cover up an ugly heart or mean-spirited words. So focus as much on the inside as the outside. Maybe more so.

The Bible is clear: this sort of beauty is "the greatest value in God's sight." There's no eyeliner that even comes close!

I will focus on my inner beauty as much as my outward beauty, Lord! Help me, I pray. Amen.

SPEAK. . .ACT!

*For the kingdom of God does not
consist in talk but in power.*
1 Corinthians 4:20 esv

The kingdom of God doesn't consist of talk, but of power. What do you think when you read those words? As a daughter of the King, do you feel powerful? (Hint: you should!)

Of course, you can't go by your feelings. But when you realize that the same God who created the whole world and everything in it created you too, you'll be more courageous!

God placed His Spirit inside of you when you gave your heart to Him. And with the Spirit comes great power. You can do things you never dreamed of doing before—like standing strong even when everyone around you is crumbling. You can make amazing, godly choices even in the face of great opposition.

That's what Esther did. She stood up during a very difficult time and didn't just speak—she acted.

You can act too. With God on your side, you can impact your world in an amazing way!

*I don't want to be known as a girl who is all talk and no
show, Lord! I don't want my tongue to say one thing and
my actions another. Give me courage to be who I say I am
and to take a stand for the things that matter. Amen.*

FAITHFUL IN MUCH

"Whoever is faithful in small matters will be faithful in large ones; whoever is dishonest in small matters will be dishonest in large ones."
LUKE 16:10 GNT

Being part of the royal family has its perks, but it also comes with an added level of responsibility. Think of the British royals. They must be very careful of what they say, what they do, where they go, who they hang out with. The media follows them and reports on their every move.

Things aren't quite as intrusive for members of Jesus' family (there are no cameras following you around), but people are watching. As soon as you say, "I'm a Christian," people start eyeing you to see if you're going to live out who you say you are.

Of course, you don't want to "behave" only because people are watching, but it does give added incentive to live right and to be consistent. The words coming out of your mouth have to match your actions and your motives.

Above all, your heavenly Father is watching. You want to bring joy to His heart with all you say and do.

*I want to honor You, Jesus! Let me be consistent
so that I can point others to You. Amen.*

DO YOU KNOW WHO YOU ARE?

I pray that out of his glorious riches he may strengthen you with power through his Spirit in your inner being, so that Christ may dwell in your hearts through faith. And I pray that you, being rooted and established in love, may have power, together with all the Lord's holy people, to grasp how wide and long and high and deep is the love of Christ.

Ephesians 3:16–18 niv

Esther understood who she was—as a person and in her faith. As a young Jewish woman, she realized that she walked in covenant (bonded relationship) with God. That bond could never be broken.

You live in covenant too. As soon as you give your heart to Him, you're His! You'll never again have to question why you were born or why you have the personality and talents that you do. All of that was ordained by God, who "covenants" with you, to always walk with you and to make you the best you can be.

The enemy of your soul wants nothing more than to distract you by having you question your identity. This is a sly trick he's using these days, hoping to throw people off track. If he can make you question who you are in Christ, you will lose your way.

Be like Esther. Understand that your identity is rooted and grounded in Christ. And He made you just as you are, to do great things for Him.

I'm rooted and grounded in You, Jesus!
Thank You for that reminder. Amen.

IDENTITY THEFT

*"The thief comes only to steal and kill and destroy; I have
come that they may have life, and have it to the full."*
JOHN 10:10 NIV

The enemy is really working overtime to make teens question their identity. These days, they're identifying as anything and everything. . .but themselves.

So why do you suppose Satan is working overtime at identity theft?

Simple. Because he knows that if you question your identity, you will question everything, including God's very existence. If Satan can make you doubt your physical body, your emotions, your very being, then he can distract you from focusing on who you are in Christ.

The Bible says your identity is in Jesus. So if someone asks, "What do you identify as?" there's really only one answer for the believer: "I identify as a Christian. I died to myself years ago when I gave my heart to Jesus. Now I live for Him only!"

Don't let the enemy rob you of your identity. You were born to be you—beautiful, wonderful you. There's no need to radically change your identity to fit in or even to make yourself feel accepted or loved. You're already accepted and loved by the very one who gave His life for you.

*My identity is in You, Jesus! I won't
let anyone steal it from me. Amen.*

GOD'S HANDIWORK

God has made us what we are, and in our union with
Christ Jesus he has created us for a life of good deeds,
which he has already prepared for us to do.
EPHESIANS 2:10 GNT

Have you ever seen a glassblower at work? It's remarkable how she takes a simple piece of glass and blows it into a gorgeous work of art. The transformation is breathtaking.

The same is true of a potter who takes a simple lump of clay and works it into a beautiful bowl or plate. The potter's handiwork is amazing.

You are like that lump of clay or that piece of glass. God has crafted you into a thing of great beauty in His eyes. You're His handiwork. (You're not a mistake, that's for sure!)

Do you see yourself as beautiful? Do you see yourself as handcrafted by the Creator? If not, then it's time to change your perspective! When you understand how much He loves you, and the great care He took to create you, it changes your perspective on pretty much everything.

You're His handiwork, created to do amazing things! Don't let this world rob you of that, girl! God prepared everything about you in advance, just as a potter or glassblower would imagine the finished product before ever starting it. You're a thing of beauty.

Help me see myself as Your handiwork, Lord!
My identity is in You and You alone. Amen.

YOU ARE A TEMPLE, GIRL!

*Don't you know that your body is the temple of the Holy
Spirit, who lives in you and who was given to you by God?
You do not belong to yourselves but to God; he bought
you for a price. So use your bodies for God's glory.*
1 Corinthians 6:19–20 gnt

Some churches are so beautiful, so colorful and exquisite, that you gasp when you walk inside of them. You're in awe of your surroundings, and it shows in how you respond. You lower your voice to speak and you walk carefully. In short, you treat the place with reverence.

Your body is just like that gorgeous church building. The Bible says that your body is a temple of the Spirit, who lives in you. When people spend time with you, they immediately feel that sense of awe you feel when you walk into a beautiful church building. There's something different about you. You're exquisite.

Oh, you might not feel like it. You might feel like a run-down shed, not an ornate temple. But the Spirit of God lives inside you, and He has made your heart His home. So trust that your identity is in Him, nothing else.

*I will honor You with my body, Jesus! You gave
everything for me. I give myself to You in return.
Thank You for living inside of me. Amen.*

FLING WIDE, O GATES!

Freedom is what we have—Christ has set us free!
Stand, then, as free people, and do not allow
yourselves to become slaves again.
GALATIANS 5:1 GNT

When is a prisoner set free from prison? When they have completed their sentence, served their time, paid their debt.

When Jesus died on the cross, He set you free from the prison of sin. He flung wide the gates of bondage and said, "This one's on Me. Now go and sin no more."

And so you walk out into the sunshine, free from the sins of your past. (Hey, you made a few mistakes along the way!)

But now what? Once Christ has set you free, He plans for you to live in that freedom from then on. So you can't let yourself get caught up in the same sins your friends and fellow students at school are involved in. Those things aren't part of God's plan for you. Sure, He can (and will) forgive you when you slip up, but do the courageous thing. Just say no to the temptations and live like a girl who has been set free from bondage once and for all.

You set me free so that I could go on living in freedom.
I get it, Lord! I won't let myself get caught in the
traps of this world anymore. My life is in You.
My identity is in You. My freedom is in You! Amen.

STICK TO THE ORIGINAL

So God created man in his own image, in the image of God
he created him; male and female he created them.
GENESIS 1:27 ESV

Imagine you were called in to paint a portrait of King Charles III. No doubt you would do your best to make the image on your canvas as close to the real person as possible.

When God created you, He painted His own image on your canvas. It's true! You're created in the image of God. Every single part of you was ordained to be just like it is. So don't fight what you look like. Don't fight the kind of personality He gave you. (Unless you're abusing it in some way, of course.)

Instead, try to stay as close to the original as you possibly can. Keep the image that you present to the world as Christlike as possible. You represent Him here on this earth, after all! So keep your identity in Him.

Thank You for painting me into Your story, Lord!
I want to represent You well! Help me do that by
making great choices every day. Amen.

BEFORE THE WORLD WAS MADE

*Even before the world was made, God had already chosen
us to be his through our union with Christ, so that we would
be holy and without fault before him. Because of his love
God had already decided that through Jesus Christ he would
make us his children—this was his pleasure and purpose.*
EPHESIANS 1:4–5 GNT

It's kind of crazy and cool to realize that God knew you before you were
born. In fact, He knew you before He ever created the world.

Don't believe it? Look at today's scripture: "Before the world was
made" you were chosen to be holy and blameless in God's sight. He
knew you would be one of His adopted kiddos before the sun, moon, and
stars floated in the sky. When you read this, how does it make you feel?

Because God always wanted you, always cared about you, always
knew you would be in relationship with Him, it's more important than
ever to honor Him with every area of your life. You weren't only chosen,
girl. You were chosen to be holy and blameless in His sight and to do
amazing things for Him.

Live up to that calling! Be brave. Be diligent and consistent. And
above all, seek Him first, above everything else. You were on His mind.
Make sure He's on yours.

*Thanks for thinking of me, Jesus. I want to
honor You with every area of my life. Amen.*

YOU ARE THE RIGHTEOUSNESS OF GOD

God made him who had no sin to be sin for us, so that
in him we might become the righteousness of God.
2 CORINTHIANS 5:21 NIV

Do you ever think about why God decided to send His Son, Jesus, to die for you? Of all people to carry the weight of the world on His shoulders, why would He send the Sinless One?

He could have chosen Satan to come and take the punishment. He deserved it, after all. Why Jesus? What did He ever do to deserve that kind of pain?

Jesus came as the ultimate example of holiness. We learn by His example that it's possible to rise above our circumstances, to love people who are unkind to us, to keep praying for things that seem impossible.

Understanding this will give you the courage to stay away from sinful activities. When you realize the overwhelming generosity of the Creator to pour Himself out for you, it will humble you on every level. So do your best to walk in the righteousness of God every day.

I will do my best to live up to this precious and holy gift
You've given me, Jesus. I'll never understand why You
loved me so much, but I'm eternally grateful. Amen.

NOTHING CAN SEPARATE ME FROM GOD'S LOVE

For I am convinced that neither death nor life, neither angels nor demons, neither the present nor the future, nor any powers, neither height nor depth, nor anything else in all creation, will be able to separate us from the love of God that is in Christ Jesus our Lord.
ROMANS 8:38–39 NIV

You've had a rough day. You said and did some things you shouldn't have. Now you're feeling bad about it all. You wish you could take it back. You wonder how God—or others—could still love you. You're a hot mess, after all. No matter how hard you try not to be.

Then you read Romans 8:38–39, and you realize the truth: nothing can separate you from God. Nothing. Not your bad attitude. Not your sin. Not your smart-aleck mouth. Not the anger in your heart.

Literally, nothing you do (or think) will ever cause God to stop loving you. It's remarkable, really. Even if you deliberately tried to break up with Jesus, it wouldn't work. He loves you that much. He forgives every time you ask. He gives second, third, fourth, and fiftieth chances.

When you understand that kind of love, it makes you want to be a better person, doesn't it?

Jesus, I don't know why You keep loving me and forgiving me, but I'm so glad You do. I'm safe and secure in Your love no matter what.

YOU ARE REDEEMED!

For he has rescued us from the dominion of darkness
and brought us into the kingdom of the Son he loves,
in whom we have redemption, the forgiveness of sins.
Colossians 1:13–14 NIV

Fifty years ago people used to collect special stamps, which they would place in books. The books of stamps would be taken to the grocery store or other businesses and swapped for products. If you had five books of stamps, you might come home with a toy or game. You would "redeem" the stamps in the store by trading them for product.

What Jesus did for you is like that. He saw every sin, every flaw, in the book of your life. Think of them as bad stamps. And He decided to trade them in for eternal life. He took something bad and swapped it for something good.

You've been redeemed, girl. God made a great trade. He gave you eternity in exchange for sin. (That's amazing!) Your Savior loves you beyond belief and would do it all over again if He had to. For now, live confidently as a child of God who has been redeemed, set free from the sins of yesterday.

Thank You for redeeming me, Jesus! You swapped
something terrible (my sin) for something wonderful
(heaven). I'm so grateful to be Your child! Amen.

NOT EVERYONE IS A FRIEND

*Repay no one evil for evil, but give thought to
do what is honorable in the sight of all. If possible,
so far as it depends on you, live peaceably with all.*
ROMANS 12:17–18 ESV

Some people pretend to be your friend, but they're not. You find out—through the grapevine or after some time together—that this person is anything but your friend. Oh, she goes through all the motions. Says the right things. But behind your back? Yeah, that's a different story.

Esther had a lot of enemies too. And some of them didn't even try to hide the truth from her. Anyone who is doing great things for God can expect to have opposition. Why? Because Satan is alive and well on planet Earth and doing everything he can to turn people against each other. He loves nothing more than to divide and conquer.

Keep your eyes wide open for people pretending to be one thing when they're really another. But also pray that God will open the door to honest, healthy friendships that will help you grow in your faith. He wants that for you, you know! And remember, you're not here to repay evil for evil. That's not how this works. You're here to live honorably in front of everyone, even the very ones who hurt you the most.

*I need good friends who can be trusted, Jesus.
Guide me to just the right ones. Thank You! Amen.*

FRIENDS IN HIGH PLACES

And the scripture was fulfilled that says,
"Abraham believed God, and it was credited to him
as righteousness," and he was called God's friend.
JAMES 2:23 NIV

- -

Some people think it's important to have "the right friends." They want to hang with the cool kids, the popular crowd, because they believe other people will see them as cool too. (In other words, they think there will be an assumption of coolness based on association.)

There might be some truth to that. If the most popular girl in school befriended you, others might start to think you were popular too. But there's so much more to friendship than association.

You already have friends in high places, girl. You're part of a heavenly kingdom, and the God of the universe is your friend. Don't believe it? Check out today's verse!

The next time you're feeling down because you don't seem to fit in, remember the truth—Jesus is more than your Savior; He's also your friend!

There are days when I feel like I have more enemies
than friends, Lord. It gets kind of lonely, to be honest.
Thank You for reminding me that You're my friend.
(And You're definitely in high places!) Amen.

POSSESSION

"If you belonged to the world, it would love you as its own. As it is, you do not belong to the world, but I have chosen you out of the world. That is why the world hates you."
JOHN 15:19 NIV

• •

Who owns you? No, really. Who owns you? When you were a little girl, it might have been fair to answer that question with the words "Well, I guess my parents do! They pay for everything." No doubt they're still paying for most things.

Here's the truth: Many "things" in this world will want to take possession of you. Friends. Agendas. Belief systems. It's up to you to not sell out. You were already purchased (at great price) by Jesus Christ when He died on the cross for you. His ownership of you is different from any other because His is born out of a deep, eternal love for you, His child.

Jesus won't treat you like a slave. According to the Bible, you are a member of the family once you give your heart to Him. You're adopted into the greatest family on earth, girl!

Don't let the world take possession of you. Stick close to Jesus. Set yourself apart for Him so that you can accomplish great things for the kingdom!

I won't let the world snag me, Jesus! I'm sticking close to You, not to the things of this world. Amen.

GASLIGHTING

Do not be deceived: "Bad company ruins good morals."
1 Corinthians 15:33 esv

Have you ever heard the term *gaslighting*?

A person who gaslights tries to make you feel like you're the problem when you're not. They are skilled in the art of manipulation and know how to make you feel guilty even when you've done absolutely nothing wrong.

Gaslighting is a special trick the enemy uses to keep people in relationships they shouldn't be in.

Maybe you can relate. Maybe you have a "friend" who gaslights you. She's always trying to manipulate you, to make you feel like you must do or say certain things to make her happy. This isn't a healthy relationship, and it's probably one you need to get out of.

She won't make it easy. Manipulators have amazing skills and know just what to say to get you to stay put. They're like puppeteers and you're the puppet. Only, it's not godly to be someone else's puppet. The Lord wants you set free from manipulative relationships like that. It's going to take courage, but let today's verse give you the boldness you need to move on, once and for all.

This is a tough one, Lord! There are people in my world who manipulate me. They put me through guilt trips if I say that I might walk away. Give me the courage to do the right thing. Amen.

GENTLE CORRECTION

"If your brother or sister sins, go and point out
their fault, just between the two of you. If they
listen to you, you have won them over."
MATTHEW 18:15 NIV

You have a friend. She seems like a great girl. Everyone loves her, even the adults. But you've caught her lying. Oh, not to you (that you know of). She lied to the teacher. Or another friend. Or her parents.

What do you do in a situation like that? Some people lie so easily that it's like nothing to them. But it matters to God. In fact, lying (bearing false witness) is so important to God that He put it in His Top Ten Not-to-Do List (the Ten Commandments).

The Bible says that if you have a problem with a brother or sister, you need to go to that person. This won't be easy, but if you see an area of your friend's life that needs correction, speak up. Not in a judgmental way of course. This isn't about judging her; it's about loving her as a Christian friend. Then give her permission to speak into your life as well. No doubt there are some things she's seeing in you that could stand correction too!

I don't like to be the one to point out flaws in others, Lord.
Help me when the situation calls for gentle correction.
And help me to be open to correction too. Amen.

PEOPLE ARE HARD

*"They will fight against you but will not overcome you,
for I am with you and will rescue you," declares the LORD.*
JEREMIAH 1:19 NIV

• •

Maybe you're at the "every time I turn around, something else bad happens" stage. Many people go through it, especially in their teen years.

Often these troubling times come because of other people. Let's face it—people aren't always easy! In fact, some are deliberately hard. They seem to work overtime to make your life difficult.

How you respond to these people is important. If you let yourself get worked up, angry, bitter, or cold, you'll pay a bigger price in the end. It will affect your health—physically and psychologically. It's better to back away from the troublemakers as much as you can while you can. Don't deliberately surround yourself with people who can't be trusted.

God has your back. He really does. And He has genuine people out there who don't have ulterior motives. Pray that He will reveal them to you so that you're surrounded by godly people who lift you up, not drag you down.

*Keep me safe, Lord! I don't want to be surrounded by
untrustworthy people! I'm so glad You have my back. Amen.*

WHOSE TEAM ARE YOU ON?

Again Jesus spoke to them, saying, "I am the light of the world. Whoever follows me will not walk in darkness, but will have the light of life."
JOHN 8:12 ESV

Whose team are you on? Maybe you didn't even realize there are "teams," but there are! There's the kingdom of darkness and the kingdom of light. Obviously, God heads up "Team Light," and Satan is on "Team Darkness," doing all he can to put out the light. It's your job to keep him from doing that!

Every day you'll have to choose all over again which team you're playing for. It takes courage to step from darkness to light, especially when those around you all seem to be playing for the other team. But following after Jesus means you stick with His team and don't bounce back and forth. (It's confusing to others when you're hypocritical, and it doesn't honor Jesus, who gave His life so that you could be on His team.)

This world can be a dark place. There will be times you feel overwhelmed and think Satan's team is bigger than God's. But remember, Satan is just a copycat. A phony. He will never have God's power or strength. Stick with the winning team even if it feels like the game is being lost. (Hint: we win in the end!)

I'll stick with You, Jesus! The kingdom of light is my team! Amen.

THE FULL ARMOR

Therefore put on the full armor of God, so that when the day of evil comes, you may be able to stand your ground, and after you have done everything, to stand.

EPHESIANS 6:13 NIV

- -

Are you wondering how to protect yourself from the enemies that keep cropping up? You can't just hide under the covers all the time, hoping they'll go away. As we've already discussed, the enemy of your soul— Satan—is alive and well and on the prowl!

So how do you handle the tough situations when people (and circumstances) come against you? The Bible gives you great instruction: "Put on the full armor of God, so that when the day of evil comes, you may be able to stand." God doesn't say "*if* the evil day comes." It's assumed. Bad days will come. Bad people will come. Bad situations will come.

But you can take up your armor and stand strong no matter what opposition you face. So put on the helmet of salvation, the breastplate of righteousness, the belt of truth, and the shoes of peace. Take up the shield of faith and the sword of the Spirit. These tools will help you fight battles, even the ones that seem impossible! And remember, if the little shepherd boy David could take down the giant Goliath with one tiny stone, how much more powerful are you with all of God's armor in place!

I don't like to fight battles, Lord. But I'll arm myself so I'm ready, just in case. You're the best protector ever, and I'm so grateful. Amen.

WICKED

For people who are wicked and deceitful have opened their mouths against me; they have spoken against me with lying tongues. With words of hatred they surround me; they attack me without cause. In return for my friendship they accuse me, but I am a man of prayer. They repay me evil for good, and hatred for my friendship.
PSALM 109:2–5 NIV

• •

You know the type: They can't wait to do evil, not good. It's like they have some sort of wicked agenda to wreak all the havoc they can in this lifetime. They're always in trouble or always trying to get away with something.

These same people lie. They cheat. They are cruel to others. And sometimes there's no reason behind it all. When you examine their lives, some of them come from normal, healthy families. Why are they so messed up?

The enemy uses all sorts of vile methods to capture people and draw them to the dark side. This is one reason you have to keep that armor on! He's tricky!

You're not going to fall for that though. And you're not giving up on the ones who are lost either. You will pray for them and keep on shining your light.

There's so much darkness, Lord. But I won't be afraid! I'll keep on praying and believing that the lost will be saved. Amen.

HEAPING COALS OF FIRE

To the contrary, "if your enemy is hungry, feed him;
if he is thirsty, give him something to drink; for by
so doing you will heap burning coals on his head."
ROMANS 12:20 ESV

No doubt you've already faced a few enemies in your life. And maybe you read today's verse and thought, *Wait. . .what? I'm supposed to be kind to my enemies?*

Kindness doesn't mean that you do what they say or that you make apologies for things you haven't done. But there's something to be said for offering kindness to someone who has hurt you. They're probably wondering, *Whoa. Why is she being so nice to me?*

And maybe, just maybe, they'll stop to think about what they've done to you. You never know where your kindness may lead.

Maybe that's what the "heaping coals of fire on their heads" line is all about. Your kindness burns them—but in a good way. And you know, a good fire always purifies whatever it touches. So let your kindness burn a pathway toward healing even if it's really, really hard.

I will do my best to be kind to others, even the ones who aren't always nice to me. Purify their hearts—and mine too. Amen.

A GODLY MENTOR

As a prisoner for the Lord, then, I urge you to live a life worthy
of the calling you have received. Be completely humble and
gentle; be patient, bearing with one another in love.
EPHESIANS 4:1–2 NIV

Have you ever wondered about the word *mentor*? In Christian circles, you hear this word a lot. A mentor is a person chosen by God or others who can help guide you through the stage you're going through.

If you started a new job at a factory, the boss would give you a mentor who already knew how to do that specific job. He would stick close to you every day until you were finally able to do the job on your own.

Mentoring comes with a lot of responsibility. A mentor knows she's being watched at all times by her mentee (the one in training). So it's very important to set a good example.

Think about the people who have served as mentors in your life. Maybe there's an older teen in your youth group who has stuck close to you, offering to pray or talk when you need a friend. Perhaps there's a teacher or other adult who's been a good role model.

Pay attention to your godly mentors! They have been placed by God "for such a time as this." You have a lot to learn, and they have a lot to teach you.

Thank You for placing people in my life to set a
godly example! I'm paying attention, Lord. Amen.

WHO ARE YOU MENTORING?

*Mordecai had a cousin named Hadassah, whom he had
brought up because she had neither father nor mother.
This young woman, who was also known as Esther, had a
lovely figure and was beautiful. Mordecai had taken her as
his own daughter when her father and mother died.*

ESTHER 2:7 NIV

In life you should always be both learning from and teaching people.
This is how it was in Esther's life. Her cousin Mordecai mentored her
all along the way.

Take a minute to examine the people in your inner circle. This
might include friends, siblings, cousins, classmates, and so on. Who is
mentoring you? Who are you mentoring?

You might say, "I'm not really mentoring anyone right now," but
that's not necessarily true. Whether you realize it or not, others are
watching you. Younger siblings. The kid next door. The kids you teach in
Sunday school or children's church. They're watching and following your
example. (Don't believe it? Listen to your younger siblings for a while
and see how many of your expressions and mannerisms they're using!)

A mentor takes on a lot of responsibility. If you're going to coach
others, you have to be open to letting them examine your life—your
actions and your words. Does this sound scary? Nah. It's just a matter
of being vulnerable, and that's a good thing.

Show me who I can mentor, Lord. Amen.

BE A LIGHTHOUSE

*When Jesus spoke again to the people, he said, "I am
the light of the world. Whoever follows me will never
walk in darkness, but will have the light of life."*
JOHN 8:12 NIV

Picture a ship's captain, guiding his ship at night. He's working with navigational tools and knows he's getting close to land. But it's dark. When he peers out over the railing of the ship, all he can see is, well, nothing.

Then suddenly a shaft of light breaks through the darkness. Off in the distance, a lighthouse sends its beam out over the water. With the help of the light, the captain now knows which way to go. He feels more secure. The light provides direction. Safety. Comfort.

This world is cloaked in darkness. All around you people are trying to figure out which way to go. They're using all sorts of navigational tools, but many of them aren't pointing them to God. In fact, they're being tugged away from truth and don't even realize it.

That's why you have to be a beacon of light, girl. Can you see how critical it is at this point in human history for girls like you to take a stand? People are veering off course and crashing.

Be a light. Be hope. Shine courageously in a way that guides people safely to shore.

*I want to be a beacon of light, Lord! Give me courage to shine
brightly even when I would rather hide my light from view. Amen.*

VULNERABLE

But he said to me, "My grace is sufficient for you, for my power is made perfect in weakness." Therefore I will boast all the more gladly of my weaknesses, so that the power of Christ may rest upon me....For when I am weak, then I am strong.

2 CORINTHIANS 12:9–10 ESV

If someone asked, "Are you vulnerable?" how would you answer the question? Maybe you're open and transparent in some areas of your life but not others. If you're going to reach this world for Christ and make a difference like Esther did, you have to be open. That's not always easy.

To make yourself available to others often means you let them in. They can see the real you with all your flaws. And when you finally cross this invisible barrier and let people see the real you, relationships get deeper. Conversations become more intense. Truths are told. Hearts are exposed.

And isn't that what God wants to happen? If you're going to be available to others, you can't put on a pretense that you have it all together. You have to be willing to say, "I don't know everything—and I've made a ton of mistakes—but I'm willing to learn and grow."

As people watch you live this way, they will become more like you in all the ways that matter.

It's not easy, Lord. In fact, it scares me to think about it. But I want to be more vulnerable around the people You've placed in my life. Help me. Amen.

IRON SHARPENS IRON

Iron sharpens iron, and one man sharpens another.
PROVERBS 27:17 ESV

Imagine you've been asked to slice up a large piece of uncooked meat. You reach into the drawer and come out with a knife that you think will do the trick. You try and try, but it won't cut through that raw beef. It's just not sharp enough.

To sharpen a knife, you have to run it through a sharpener. It makes that dull edge super sharp. Only then is the tool in your hand worth what you paid for it.

The same is true with your faith. If you don't keep it sharp, it will grow dull and you'll fall away. (Hey, it happens to people all the time. Those who were once strong become weak when they're not held accountable.)

Oh, you might still believe in God, but you won't have the passion you once did. That's why godly friendships are so important. Friends are the "sharpener" you need to keep your faith strong! So choose carefully, girl! You need friends who will help you become the best you that you can be!

*I need "sharp" friends, Lord! Point me
toward the right ones, I pray. Amen.*

RELIABLE PEOPLE

Take the teachings that you heard me proclaim in
the presence of many witnesses, and entrust them to
reliable people, who will be able to teach others also.
2 Timothy 2:2 GNT

Part of being courageous is passing on the good news to others. You can do this in many ways, but one of the least intimidating is by volunteering at your church to work in the children's department.

Kids today need great mentors, and you have a lot to share. After all, you've already lived a lot longer than all the little ones you'll see in church. So why not volunteer? Maybe you can help the kids sing or do motions to worship songs. Maybe you can help with crafts or snacks. Perhaps you could teach a Bible lesson or do a fun illustration.

No matter how you end up helping, just know that your very presence is also a help. You're giving those kids someone to look up to. Just make sure you're the same in and out of the classroom. You don't want them to see you praising Jesus in their class but taking His name in vain in the restroom or hallway. (See how quickly their little impressionable minds could be swayed in the wrong direction?)

"Proclaim in the presence of many witnesses." Share the love of Jesus with those kiddos, and they will help you grow in your faith too!

Show me how I can serve others, Lord. I want
to pass on the message of Your love. Amen.

CROSSING GENERATIONAL LINES

*What you have done will be praised from one generation
to the next; they will proclaim your mighty acts.*
PSALM 145:4 GNT

When you think of your friend group, does a certain demographic come to mind? Are they all female? All in their teens?

This might come as a shock to you, but God wants you to befriend people in other demographics too. It's important that you have relationships with adults (even seniors) and little kids too.

Why do you suppose it matters to the Lord that people cross generational lines to maintain good and healthy relationships? Because, as today's scripture says, the testimony of what God has done is passed down through the generations. Your grandparents, if they're still living, probably have some remarkable stories. So do your parents and your aunts and uncles.

You have great stories too. And the little ones in your life (siblings or kids you teach at church) need to hear them. So keep this generational thing going! Don't be so selective about your friend groups. Broaden your horizons, girl!

*Show me how to befriend people of different ages and stages,
Lord. I have so much to learn. . .and so much to teach! Amen.*

WHO ARE YOU WALKING WITH?

Whoever walks with the wise becomes wise,
but the companion of fools will suffer harm.
PROVERBS 13:20 ESV

If someone stopped you on the sidewalk and asked, "Who are you walking with?" how would you answer the question? It would totally depend on who you happened to be walking with at the time, right?

That "who are you walking with?" question is a legitimate one. God wants you to walk with people who are wise. The minute you link arms with foolish people, bad things start happening. You often end up going along with things you shouldn't. And sometimes you pay a heavy price just for your association with fools.

When you walk with wise people, however, your credibility level goes up. Your ability to reason properly goes up. Your decision-making skills go up. Wise people attract other wise people.

The interesting thing is you get to choose. It takes courage to choose wisdom over foolishness. (Let's face it—foolish things are sometimes funny and seem innocent at first.) But ultimately, you want to stay safe. And hanging out with wise people is one way to ensure that.

I want to stay safe, Lord, so I'll stay away from the foolish people.
They won't be my companions. I'll stick to the wise ones. Amen.

MONKEY SEE, MONKEY DO

And you should imitate me, just as I imitate Christ.
1 CORINTHIANS 11:1 NLT

• •

Monkey see, monkey do. This is an old expression that goes back many years! Even animals learn how to copycat. You see it all the time if you go to the zoo. One monkey swings on the tree; another one follows.

It's true with humans too! For example, children tend to copy the people who are raising them—parents, siblings, aunts, uncles, and so on. They do whatever is demonstrated by the older ones in their lives. And their eyes are wide open. They see the good things you do, as well as the not so good!

How does it make you feel, knowing you're being so closely watched by the young ones in your world? That places a lot of responsibility squarely on your shoulders. More than anything, it should make you want to imitate Christ so that those imitating you are getting the best possible example.

I'm not always the best example, Jesus. There are days when I mess up badly and others see it. Please forgive me and help me to do better. I really do want to be a mentor to those who are younger than me. Amen.

HUMBLE YOURSELF

Likewise, you who are younger, be subject to the elders.
Clothe yourselves, all of you, with humility toward one
another, for "God opposes the proud but gives grace to the
humble." Humble yourselves, therefore, under the mighty
hand of God so that at the proper time he may exalt you,
casting all your anxieties on him, because he cares for you.
1 PETER 5:5–7 ESV

Here's a hard truth: teenagers often think they know everything. Maybe you know someone like that. She's always snapping back at the teacher or her parents, saying, "I already knew that."

God wants your teachable spirit to remain, and He wants you to be open to learning from people of all ages. Older folks have a lot to teach you. Other teens probably have a few things to teach you. And, for sure, your parents and teachers are there to impart wisdom.

So humble yourself, girl. It might not be easy to make yourself teachable, but that's what Esther had to do under her cousin's supervision. She had to trust that this older man knew a few things she did not! Then she had to follow his lead to get the job done.

God will give you grace as you humble yourself, and that's a very good thing!

I get it, Jesus! I won't be a know-it-all. I'll have a teachable
spirit no matter who You send to teach me. Amen.

STANDING FIRM

*Therefore, put on every piece of God's armor so you
will be able to resist the enemy in the time of evil.
Then after the battle you will still be standing firm.*
EPHESIANS 6:13 NLT

Esther didn't have to do what she did. Think about that for a moment. She could have closed her eyes to what was going on with the persecution of her people. She could have said, "Well, I'm safe in the palace, so what does it matter to me what happens to them?"

The truth is she chose to do the hard thing. And let's face it—the right thing is very often the hard thing. She chose to stand up for what was right instead of sitting quietly by, letting it happen while turning a blind eye.

Maybe you've been there. You're comfortable. You're safe. You don't have to get involved. But something is tugging at your heart, and you know you must take a stand.

God will honor your courage when you stand, girl. So don't turn a blind eye. Don't look away. Look that problem squarely in the eye—even if it doesn't affect you personally—and stand up.

*It's easier not to stand, Jesus. I don't always feel like doing the right
thing. But I want to be like Esther. I don't want to turn a blind eye.
Give me the courage to stand even if I don't feel like it. Amen.*

ITCHING EARS

For a time is coming when people will no longer listen to sound and wholesome teaching. They will follow their own desires and will look for teachers who will tell them whatever their itching ears want to hear. They will reject the truth and chase after myths.
2 Timothy 4:3–4 nlt

The Bible says that in the last days people will have itching ears. They'll be looking for teachers who will tell them whatever they want to hear.

These people aren't looking for the truth. They're not looking for life-changing answers. They just want you to confirm what they already believe or think.

These people aren't teachable. More than that, they're only interested in fantasies, not reality. They wouldn't admit the truth if it was staring them in the face. They want to go on believing nonsense but insist you agree with them.

Don't do it. Don't deviate from truth to speak a lie, just to satisfy itching ears. Don't chase after myths. Don't accept fiction as reality. Instead, stand firm in the truth of God's Word even if everyone around you crumbles.

I don't want to have itching ears, Lord. I want my life to be rooted in truth. Reality, not fiction, is my friend. So when people make up crazy myths, I won't buy into them. I'll simply go on believing Your Word. Amen.

BE THE LONE PIN

That you may be blameless and innocent, children of God
without blemish in the midst of a crooked and twisted
generation, among whom you shine as lights in the world.
PHILIPPIANS 2:15 ESV

It's not easy to stand when everyone around you is falling, is it? Imagine a bowling ball hurling down the lane. It hits the center pin, and all the pins fall except one. That lone pin wobbles back and forth, as if asking, *Am I going to go down too?*

Sometimes you feel like that lone bowling pin. You're watching your friends tumble all around you, giving in to the temptation to do the wrong thing, believe the wrong thing, say the wrong thing. And you're shaken, in part because you're so startled that some of them didn't stand strong when you thought (and hoped) they would.

Be the lone pin. Even if it's hard. Be blameless and innocent before God, without blemish in the middle of a crooked and twisted generation. Shine like a light. Go on standing even if every single person around you falls.

And don't worry about what others will think about you. That's not your problem. You need to be more concerned about what God thinks about you anyway.

I get it, Jesus. It's not easy to keep standing strong when
others are falling, but You want me to give it my best. I want
to be a guiding light, so keep me standing, I pray. Amen.

SEPARATE FROM THE WORLD

Do not love the world or the things in the world. If anyone loves the world, the love of the Father is not in him. For all that is in the world—the desires of the flesh and the desires of the eyes and pride of life—is not from the Father but is from the world. And the world is passing away along with its desires, but whoever does the will of God abides forever.

1 John 2:15–17 esv

It's not easy to separate yourself from the world, is it? You want to love all the things your friends love: movies, clothes, culture trends, and so on.

But the Bible is clear: it's important not to get too attached to the world or the things in it. Why do you suppose that is? Why does God encourage you to hold the world at arm's length and not cuddle it close?

The world is filled with temptations that seek to separate you from God. Travel too far down any of those temptation-driven roads and you'll find yourself seeking after them, not Him.

He wants you to seek Him first. And the Lord (who adores you) will give you all the other "things" that you need to be satisfied and fulfilled. He's not out to ruin your plans or put a damper on your joy.

Trust Him. The things He wants to give you are eternal, girl. They won't fade to dust like the things of this crazy old world.

I get it, Jesus! Anything the world offers is temporary.
You have eternal gifts for me that are so much better. Amen.

STICK CLOSE TO JESUS

For people will be lovers of self, lovers of money, proud, arrogant, abusive, disobedient to their parents, ungrateful, unholy.
2 Timothy 3:2 esv

The Bible tells us that in the last days people will start acting very strangely. It's almost like they'll lose their minds (or lose their way). They'll think more about themselves than others. They'll run after money and the things it can offer. They'll be prideful (one of the seven deadly sins). They will be arrogant, stuck-up. (You won't be able to teach them anything.) These people will have some anger and treat others abusively. Some of these people in the end-times will be disobedient to their parents. Others won't be grateful for the things they have. They'll always be craving more, more, more. And still others will be unholy.

Look at the people you know. How many of them struggle with these things? Probably quite a few! Some people speculate that we're living in the end-times, because humanity is becoming more and more like this scripture.

Regardless, strive to be the opposite. Be a lover of others. Don't chase after money. Don't be prideful or stuck-up. Don't abuse others. Treat your parents lovingly and be grateful for all you have. And above all, stick close to Jesus so that His holiness can rub off on you!

I want to be more like You, Jesus. Help me stay focused on You, not this world. Amen.

SPEAK UP!

For the Spirit God gave us does not make us timid,
but gives us power, love and self-discipline.
2 TIMOTHY 1:7 NIV

• •

God didn't create you to be a coward. You might be shy. You might not like to speak up in a group. But even if it's not in your personality to be a showboat, you're still not intended to be like the Cowardly Lion when it comes to the things that matter.

Imagine if all the believers on the planet refused to speak up. What if no one ever said, "Now, wait a minute. That's not what the Bible says"? If no one spoke truth, lies would prevail. People wouldn't have a solid rock to stand on if no one shared the gospel.

You have to be brave even when it's hard. God didn't make you timid. He gave you internal power and fortitude, fueled by His love and His discipline. So square those shoulders. Speak truth even when it's really, really hard. Maybe God has made you to be an Esther in this generation, a girl who is going to turn things around for her people!

Sometimes I don't feel like speaking up, God. I'd rather
hide in the shadows and let someone else do the hard
work. But I will do what You've called me to do. I'll be
a voice even when no one else speaks up. Amen.

DON'T BE WISHY-WASHY

Therefore, my dear brothers and sisters, stand firm. Let nothing move you. Always give yourselves fully to the work of the Lord, because you know that your labor in the Lord is not in vain.
1 Corinthians 15:58 niv

* *

Always means always. And, if we're honest, *always* is *sometimes* a hard word for us to live out. We don't always feel like cleaning our rooms. We don't always feel like being nice to that pesky sibling. We don't always feel like eating healthy foods or doing the dishes.

In today's verse, we read that God wants us to "always" give ourselves to His work. *Always* means without interruption. So, when you're in school, you're working for God. When you're playing sports, you're doing it all for Him. When you're at a family get-together, He's right there, at the center of it.

It changes your entire perspective to see that everything you say, do, or plan is to be centered on Christ, doesn't it? And yet that's the truth. Always give everything to Him. Every word. Every action. Every relationship.

And while you're at it, stand firm! Don't be wishy-washy, grumbling about all you have to do for God. Be bold, and go for it all with great gusto in your heart. What a difference maker you will be, girl!

I will always be on Your team, Jesus! Nothing will move me away from You. I give all my plans to You. Amen.

HARDER THAN BEFORE

But understand this, that in the last days there will come times of difficulty. For people will be lovers of self, lovers of money, proud, arrogant, abusive, disobedient to their parents, ungrateful, unholy, heartless, unappeasable, slanderous, without self-control, brutal, not loving good, treacherous, reckless, swollen with conceit, lovers of pleasure rather than lovers of God, having the appearance of godliness, but denying its power. Avoid such people.
2 Timothy 3:1–5 esv

Does life seem harder than ever before? The Bible says that in the last days there will be times of difficulty. If you read today's verses, you'll find a long, long list of things you can expect to see in the last days.

"Last days" could refer to dozens or even hundreds of years. No one really knows. But it would seem, based on the list, that we're in that era known as "last days."

So how do you live with courage during tumultuous times? First, stand apart from worldly people who live like those described in this passage from 2 Timothy. Don't buy into their teachings or beliefs. (The world's belief system is always broken and twisted.)

Next, keep shining your light. You can do this by standing firm on the Bible. The words you'll find there will keep you going strong.

I will do my best no matter how hard things get, Jesus. With You walking alongside me, I can tackle anything! Amen.

YOU'RE BETTER THAN THAT!

Do not love the world or the things in the world. If anyone loves the world, the love of the Father is not in him.

1 John 2:15 esv

. . . .

It takes courage not to fall in love with the things of this world. They're quite tempting, after all. Many people in your age group fall in love with someone and allow relationships to go too far. Others fall for notoriety. Others get wrapped up in their talents and abilities and do all they can to show those off. Some people chase after money.

It takes courage not to follow the crowd. It takes a tremendous amount of confidence in God to look at the things of this world and say, "Yeah, that's nice, but I have something better."

You *do* have something better. All the fame this life can give doesn't begin to compare to the joy of spending eternity with God. Even if you won the lottery and had millions of dollars, it wouldn't come close to the streets of gold and gates of pearl you'll one day see in heaven. And even the finest friendship here on earth can't compare to spending time with the King of the universe.

Having stuff is okay. It's okay to have success. But remember, none of those things should be more important than your relationship with God.

I won't love this world or the things in it, Jesus! I'll put You first in all I do. Amen.

IT'S BETTER TO GIVE
THAN RECEIVE

*"In all things I have shown you that by working hard in this way
we must help the weak and remember the words of the Lord Jesus,
how he himself said, 'It is more blessed to give than to receive.'"*
ACTS 20:35 ESV

Maybe you've heard the expression "It's better to give than to receive." No doubt you thought it was talking about money or material possessions.

Take a closer look at the first part of the verse: "In all things I have shown you that by working hard in this way we must help the weak."

Wow. So maybe the "giving" isn't just about handing someone some money or a free lunch. Maybe God is trying to get at something bigger and more important here. Could it be that what He wants you to give is your time? Your energy? Your mentoring?

What if God interrupted your daily plan and said, "Okay, today, instead of going over to your friend's house to hang out, there's this new girl at school who needs a friend. I want you to reach out to her to ask if she needs anything."

You never know, do you? Maybe your words will be just what she needs on a critical day.

*Use me, God. I make myself available—to help others and to listen
to those Holy Spirit nudges to be an encouragement. Amen.*

BE A GAP CLOSER

*On the third day Esther put on her royal robes and stood in the
inner court of the palace, in front of the king's hall. The king was
sitting on his royal throne in the hall, facing the entrance. When
he saw Queen Esther standing in the court, he was pleased with
her and held out to her the gold scepter that was in his hand.
So Esther approached and touched the tip of the scepter.*
ESTHER 5:1–2 NIV

Esther faced what was surely the most difficult decision of her life when
she was asked by her cousin to approach the king on behalf of the Jewish
people. If the king heard her request and granted it, she would save her
people. If he turned her away, she could very easily lose her own life.

Esther garnered the strength to approach the king in his throne room.
She must have approached with fear and trembling, but every step she
took was a step to close the gap between her people and their rescue.

Because of her courage, the gap was closed, her people were saved,
and the king's mind was completely changed. All because one girl took
a chance and broke down the wall between them.

You can be like Esther. You can be a gap closer. Every time you pray
for someone, you're helping close the gap between that person and God.
Lives can be changed if you step up and approach the King on their behalf.

*I will be a gap closer, Jesus. I will pray for my friends and loved
ones who need to know You. I know I don't have to be afraid to
approach You, Lord! You will never turn me away. Amen.*

STAND BY THE ROADS

Thus says the LORD: "Stand by the roads, and look, and ask
for the ancient paths, where the good way is; and walk in it,
and find rest for your souls. But they said, 'We will not walk in it.'"
JEREMIAH 6:16 ESV

Have you ever been in a prayer circle? People gather all around the room and hold hands, forming a complete ring.

Sometimes people are spread out too far and their hands don't reach. So everyone must move in a little to make it work. They must fill in the gaps so that hands and hearts can be linked.

Now think about the people you know who are out on the fringes. They seem lost, lonely, and afraid. No one is making room for them in the circle. No one is standing in the gap.

Sometimes God wants you to be the one to fill in the empty spaces between that person and a relationship with Jesus Christ. He wants you to step in that person's pathway and say, "I'm here. I'll show you the way."

Stand by the roads. Walk in the good way. And bring others with you so that they can one day experience the joy of heaven too.

I'll stand in the gap for others, Jesus. I won't give up on them even
when their situations seem hopeless. Show me how to stand in faith
even when it makes no sense to go on standing and believing. Amen.

NO COUCH POTATOES IN BATTLE

Stand therefore, having girded your loins with truth,
and having put on the breastplate of righteousness.
EPHESIANS 6:14 RSV

What a strange verse, right? What are a person's loins, anyway?

If you were going to the butcher to buy a great cut of meat, you might ask for loin meat. It's the part between the highest point on the hip bone to the lowest rib.

In humans, loins are also the part of your anatomy below the ribs and down to the hip bone. Basically, what we would call our abdomen. Some might even say stomach, but loins wouldn't technically include that organ.

So why "gird" your loins when you're standing firm? Basically, the Lord is telling us to prepare ourselves for stressors. They're coming, and we need to be ready. A battle is on the way, and if you tighten your midsection as you prepare, you won't be caught being lazy or sloppy. There are no couch potatoes in the heat of battle, after all. Only those who are prepared will go on to do great things for God.

I'm not a big fan of battles, Lord, but I've faced a lot of them,
and I feel like more are coming. Thanks for the reminder to stand
firm and strong so that I'm ready when the time comes. Amen.

SUPERNATURAL PEACE

When a man's ways please the LORD, he makes
even his enemies to be at peace with him.
PROVERBS 16:7 ESV

• •

Don't you just love the promise from today's verse? When you walk in a way that's pleasing to the Lord, He does something supernatural—He causes the very people who've tormented and hated you to live at peace with you.

Whoa. That's big. Maybe you're being harassed by someone who causes you grief every day at school. If you want this person to leave you alone, draw near to God. Live in a way that brings joy to His heart. Learn how to respond in love even when it's hard. Don't make the problem worse by overreacting.

In other words, figure out a way to live in peace even if this other person won't quit. Because, once you quiet your spirit and give the situation to God, He really will take care of it. You just never know how He might turn things around.

I'll do my best to live the way You want me to, Lord. I would be so
excited if my enemies would calm down and go away! Amen.

WALL BUILDERS

*"I looked for someone who could build a wall, who could stand
in the places where the walls have crumbled and defend the land
when my anger is about to destroy it, but I could find no one."*

Ezekiel 22:30 GNT

. . . .

What would happen if all the protective walls around an ancient city fell down? It would be vulnerable to the enemy's attacks, right? The same is true with spiritual walls. If solid theology crumbles, then what rises in its place? Lies, of course.

God is looking for wall builders, people who will guard and protect the faith and His people. He wants you to keep standing for truth even when it feels impossible.

Today, when beliefs seem to be eroding, when people seem to follow whatever they want to follow, you can be the one who stands firm, filling in the gap in the broken-down places. You can be the one to say, "I'm standing for truth, not a lie."

There are people who are looking for someone to do the right thing. Be that someone.

*I can see that the walls of what people believe about
You are crumbling, Lord. I will stand in the gap and
show them that You haven't changed. You're the
same—yesterday, today, and forever. Amen.*

THE POT'S BOILING OVER!

Trust in the LORD with all your heart, and do not lean on your own understanding. In all your ways acknowledge him, and he will make straight your paths.

PROVERBS 3:5–6 ESV

In all your ways, acknowledge Him. Okay, let's get real: that's a tough one. When you're in the middle of a fight with your mom? When your sister is driving you nuts? During the last five minutes of an impossible exam?

Even in all those times, trust in the Lord with all your heart and lean not on your own understanding? Is that even possible?

Humans have what's called a fight-or-flight response to most calamities. (And let's face it—a tough exam can feel like a calamity.) During those crazy moments when your stress level is building, building, building, it takes great courage and peace of mind to stop, take a few deep breaths, and whisper, "Even now, Jesus. You're in charge. Take over."

He will, you know. Even then, when the emotional pot is about to boil over. You're just a few deep breaths away from making the right decision.

Place your trust in the Lord. . .in all your ways. Every. Single. One.

Whew! This is a tough one, Jesus! When I'm in the heat of the moment, I will pause, take a breath, and turn to You. My trust won't be in myself but in You alone. Amen.

DROP THOSE WEIGHTS!

It is for freedom that Christ has set us free. Stand firm, then,
and do not let yourselves be burdened again by a yoke of slavery.
GALATIANS 5:1 NIV

• •

Did you ever wonder why Jesus went to all the trouble He did to come live a sinless life and then face the cross with the weight of your sin on His shoulders?

Some people would say, "So that I could live in heaven!" And that's an appropriate answer, of course. But Jesus doesn't want our days here on earth to be weighed down with unnecessary things. He came to set us free—from the emotional baggage, the shame of yesterday, the sins that once held us bound.

He came to offer freedom to captives and sight to the blind, not just to give a free pass into heaven. So if you're feeling like the weight you're carrying is too much, remember: Jesus came to relieve you of that. Your shoulders aren't big enough. It's going to take courage to release your burdens and place them in His hands, but He can handle them. In fact, He died for that very reason.

You want to set me free from the things that keep me from
running my race, Jesus. I've carried so much guilt and
shame, so many hang-ups and so much inner turmoil. Today
I do the brave thing and release those into Your capable
hands. Only You can carry them, Lord. Not me. Amen.

HOLD FAST TO THE FAITH

So then, brothers, stand firm and hold to the traditions that you
were taught by us, either by our spoken word or by our letter.
2 Thessalonians 2:15 esv

Does your family have any traditions? Maybe you always go to the same place for Thanksgiving or Christmas dinner. Maybe you always take vacations in the same place. Maybe your mom (or dad) loves to cook the same meal repeatedly. These familiar things can be comforting. You get used to them and come to expect them.

There are traditions of the faith too. Going to church and worshipping with fellow believers. Offering up your heart in worship alongside others of like faith. Giving. Helping. Taking Communion. These are all things that have come down from one generation to another.

God loves it when you keep many of those things going—not out of rote (vain repetition) but out of sheer love for Him and for others. Church can be fun, especially when you go with the intention of meeting Jesus there and of encouraging and building up your friends.

Hold fast to the faith. Don't give it up because you're feeling lazy or tired. God wants you to be all in, girl!

May all the things I do bring joy to Your heart,
Jesus, and grow me into a stronger Christian. Amen.

INTERCESSION

Likewise the Spirit helps us in our weakness. For we do not know what to pray for as we ought, but the Spirit himself intercedes for us with groanings too deep for words. And he who searches hearts knows what is the mind of the Spirit, because the Spirit intercedes for the saints according to the will of God.
ROMANS 8:26–27 ESV

Have you ever been so worked up that your words didn't come out right? Maybe you were facing a crisis of some sort and couldn't seem to string together the right words to tell your parents or teacher what was going on, because you were too shaken up.

In those moments when words won't come, you can completely rely on the Holy Spirit to intercede (pray) for you. He's right there, with groanings too deep for words. You've probably had times when all you could do was groan or cry out.

Let the Lord search your heart. Let Him speak on your behalf. And let Him carry the load when it's just too big or too heavy to lift by yourself.

I don't always know what to say, Jesus. There are times when I'm so overwhelmed that words won't come. But I can trust the Holy Spirit to speak on my behalf, praying God's will over my scary situation. I trust You, Lord! Amen.

HOVERING OVER THE DARKNESS

*In the beginning, when God created the universe,
the earth was formless and desolate. The raging ocean
that covered everything was engulfed in total darkness,
and the Spirit of God was moving over the water.*
GENESIS 1:1–2 GNT

. . . .

Somewhere in the vastness of the formless, desolate earth, an ocean raged. Before the days of man. Before the days of light and dark. Before crickets sang their evening song or puppies lapped at bowls of water. . .

Before all of that there was a formless, desolate place that would one day teem with life. And there, in the gap between "In the beginning" and all that would come after, the Holy Spirit moved across the waters.

Right there, in the middle of creation's story, God's Spirit hovered. And danced like the morning breeze—before there was a breeze to dance on.

The Spirit of God refused to remain stagnant even when darkness reigned. And He won't remain stagnant when you're facing dark times either.

He's right there—the comforter, your friend, the very essence of courage and power. No matter what you're facing today, the Spirit of God is moving, just as He did during creation.

*Thank You, Lord, for sending Your Holy Spirit
to bring power and comfort to my life! Amen.*

A WORTHY MANNER

*Whatever happens, conduct yourselves in
a manner worthy of the gospel of Christ.*
PHILIPPIANS 1:27 NIV

Imagine you are in the military. Like all the other recruits, you wear the same uniform, speak the way they speak, and behave as instructed. You don't dare deviate from protocol for fear of being ousted.

Thankfully, you'll never be ousted from God's army, but that doesn't mean you can march to your own drumbeat. You still have to conduct yourself in a manner worthy of the gospel. It wouldn't do for one core member to go off on a tangent and do something crazy (or break the rules on purpose). It gives the whole group a bad name.

That's kind of how it is when you say you're a Christian but don't live like it. You're in the core group, but you're not conducting yourself in a worthy manner.

Ultimately, God cares about your heart. It's not about rules with Him. He wants you to follow His commands so that you can have a healthy, productive life! And, along the way, you'll bring others to Him if they see your authentic relationship with Christ.

*I will conduct myself in a worthy manner, Jesus! I will follow
hard after You and share authentically with others. Amen.*

A GOOD NAME

*A good name is to be chosen rather than great
riches, and favor is better than silver or gold.*
PROVERBS 22:1 ESV

Why do you suppose God cares so much about His children having a good name? Lots of people mess up, right? Reputations are destroyed every day because of bad choices. God forgives and forgets, so why all this stuff about having a good name? No one is perfect, after all!

Here's the thing: God wants you to try. He doesn't want you to go out of your way to ruin your reputation, because you are a representative of Him on this earth.

Not sure how that works? Imagine that a door-to-door salesman comes to your door with a handy-dandy cleaning product. You tell him you're not interested and try to close the door. He gets angry and starts to cuss you out. You slam the door and proclaim, "I'll never buy that product no matter what!"

That salesman damaged the name of his company, didn't he? And that's kind of what happens when you deliberately live in sin while claiming to be a believer. You sully the name of Christ with your actions. It brings dishonor to Him and shame to you. So do your best to represent Him well. Keep that good name, girl!

*I will do my best to bring honor to You, Jesus!
I will represent You well. Amen.*

THEY WILL SEE YOUR GOOD DEEDS

Your conduct among the heathen should be so good that when they accuse you of being evildoers, they will have to recognize your good deeds and so praise God on the Day of his coming.

1 PETER 2:12 GNT

• •

Do you ever feel like you're wasting your time living a holy life when everyone around you is doing their own thing, completely forgetting about God? Even some people who claim to be Christians don't seem to be living up to the name. Sad, right?

Here's the thing though: Those people (whether you recognize it or not) are paying attention to how you live. They see when you refuse to participate in activities that don't honor God. Oh, they might make fun of you in the moment, but secretly they are admiring your courage and strength to do the right thing.

And check out today's verse! When you live for Jesus and represent Him well (something that takes great courage in today's culture), people will recognize your good deeds and eventually praise God.

So don't give up. It's not a waste of time. It's not in vain. Keep standing strong so that others can come to know the Lord too.

By the power of Your Holy Spirit within me, I'll go on living in a way that glorifies You, Lord! I won't give in to the temptation to do what people around me are doing. I'll march to Your drumbeat, not theirs! Amen.

RISKING YOUR REPUTATION

He always had the nature of God, but he did not think that by force he should try to remain equal with God. Instead of this, of his own free will he gave up all he had, and took the nature of a servant. He became like a human being and appeared in human likeness.

PHILIPPIANS 2:6–7 GNT

When you hear the word *reputation*, what comes to mind? If you have a particular talent or ability, you might be known for that. For instance, people might say, "Oh, Chelsea? She has such an amazing voice. You should hear her sing!"

When Esther (who was a gorgeous young Jewish woman) approached the king, she had a reputation as queen. But she also had a reputation among the Jewish people as one of them. So when she decided to risk everything to represent her people to the king, it was a big deal!

Maybe you've done things that risked your reputation too. Perhaps you spoke up about your faith and wondered if people would ridicule you or criticize your differences. Maybe you went out of your way to treat a bullied student with kindness.

It can be a good thing to mess up your reputation *if* you're performing an act of kindness. Don't worry so much about what others think, girl. Be more concerned with what God thinks.

I get it, Lord! My reputation is important, but I can't let what other people think about me be the most important thing. I only care what You think, Jesus! Amen.

THE SHADOWS OF DARKNESS

*Even though I walk through the valley of the shadow
of death, I will fear no evil, for you are with me;
your rod and your staff, they comfort me.*
PSALM 23:4 ESV

Picture yourself in a place of great darkness—a deep valley with mountains on either side of you. No sun can shine down on that place. Walking forward is difficult with the shadows blocking your view.

Even there, in that dark and hidden place, God is with you. No matter what you're going through. No matter how hard it seems. The one who created you and knows you best is as close as your nearest breath.

There's no reason to fear—even when the shadows of darkness settle in around you. Your Good Shepherd will still guide you out of those shadows and into the light. So hold tight to His hand. Be courageo Allow Him to keep you moving even when you don't feel like it.

Sometimes I freeze
g
n locked
Your presence.
You bring me comfort
. Thank You, Lord! Amen.

NO OBSTACLES

We put no obstacle in anyone's way, so that
no fault may be found with our ministry.
2 CORINTHIANS 6:3 ESV

Have you ever heard someone say, "Don't be a stumbling block"? What's a stumbling block anyway? And why would anyone ever call you that?

Picture an Olympic runner blazing down the track, moving like the wind. He's doing great until he comes to a giant hurdle that he must leap over before he can continue the race.

A stumbling block is like that hurdle. It's placed there to trip up the runner.

Have you ever met someone who claimed to be a Christian but didn't live like it? She partied just like the nonbelievers. Cussed just like them. Cheated just like them.

That girl? She's a hurdle. A stumbling block. She's giving Jesus (and Christians) a bad name. Whether she means to do it or not, she's tripping people up. And many new believers can get very confused when they meet up with people like her. After all, they're trying their best to run a clean race!

Don't be a stumbling block. Be who you say you are. Represent Christ well.

I don't want to trip anyone up with my actions, Lord! I don't want to
be a stumbling block. Remove any hypocrisy from me, I pray. Amen.

GOOD FRUIT

"A good tree produces good fruit,
and a bad tree produces bad fruit."
MATTHEW 7:17 NLT

Have you ever planted a fruit tree? Maybe you have a couple of orange trees in your backyard. One produces delicious, juicy oranges. The other one? Not so much. The few oranges it produces are hard and inedible. Why? What's the difference?

There can be several reasons why a tree doesn't produce fruit—for example, bad soil, a poor root system, or insect infestations.

The same is true for believers. Some have amazing root systems that run deep. They stay well watered and produce tasty fruit for the kingdom of God. Others have shallow roots and let themselves get dried out. Their fruit is bad in comparison.

Which of those two trees are you? Take an honest inventory. Are you pro_____ _____ _____courage to admit that you need to go deeper in your relationship with Him, _____ _____th it! And remember, the best fruit of all is the joy you'll receive once you fully and totally give your heart to God and make yourself usable.

I want to be ____ed by You, God. I want to produce good fruit.
Help m__ __ dig my roots way down deep in You! Amen.

BE REASONABLE

Let your reasonableness be known
to everyone. The Lord is at hand.
PHILIPPIANS 4:5 ESV

Would people say that you are reasonable? Are you able to talk things out with friends and family and come to an understanding even when disagreements arise?

If you've ever been around an unreasonable person, you know how tense things can get. He's always right. He's unteachable. He demands his own way. These people are tough to work with and even tougher to live with!

Being reasonable is a God trait. Isaiah 1:18 (ESV) says, "Come now, let us reason together." In other words, let's sit down and talk this out in a calm, collected way.

You might not ever agree with the person sitting across from you, but at least reasoning things out keeps walls from going up. If the world would reason things out, riots wouldn't happen. Wars would cease. Social media would calm down.

Be a part of the solution, not a part of the problem. Be reasonable, girl.

I don't want to be known as stubborn and unreasonable,
Lord. Show me, even in the moment of a heated argument,
how to bring honor to You by being reasonable. Amen.

BAD FRUIT

The name of the righteous is used in blessings,
but the name of the wicked will rot.
PROVERBS 10:7 NIV

Have you ever accidentally left food out overnight? Maybe you cut up some fruit and meant to eat it but left it in a bowl on the counter instead. What happens to food that's left out? It begins to break down—to rot. And boy, does rotting ever create a stench!

Rotten food isn't good for anyone, and neither are people who've earned a rotten name! Those stinkers give other Christians a bad name because of their behavior. Oh, they still play the game. They sit out on the counter with the rest of the lovely fruit and try to pass themselves off as healthy, but they're not!

Hang around a rotten person and you run the risk of getting spoiled too. People who say bad things about them will eventually be saying those same things about you. So make sure your name is healthy and strong. There's no room for rotting in the kingdom of God!

I don't want to give off a stench, Lord. I don't want
people to walk by me and say, "Yeah, she tries to act like
a Christian, but you should see what she's really like."
I want to be known by my good, tasty fruit. Amen.

WELL THOUGHT OF

Moreover, he must be well thought of by outsiders, so that
he may not fall into disgrace, into a snare of the devil.
1 Timothy 3:7 esv

It looks like God really cares a lot about how we're perceived by others. Why do you think that is? In today's verse, we see that He even cares about how outsiders (those outside the faith or your circle of friends) view you.

If someone said, "Hey, I know _____ (insert your name). She's really _____," how would they fill in that last blank? What are the first words that come to mind?

If a new girl joined your friend group at school, what would be her take on you? It's interesting to think about, right? Would she say, "She was really welcoming and kind." Or would she say, "Yeah, I didn't get a great vibe from that one."

You don't have to get too wound up about this. In other words, you don't need to turn into a people pleaser. That's not the point. You simply have to love others the way you want to be loved. (Hey, where have we heard that one before?) When you do things God's way, you'll always give off good vibes!

I want to be well thought of by others, Lord. I know that
starts with being genuine and by loving You first then loving
others as I love myself. Help me do that, I pray. Amen.

A SACRIFICIAL LIFE

The sacrifices of God are a broken spirit; a broken
and contrite heart, O God, you will not despise.
PSALM 51:17 ESV

Life is filled with sacrificial moments. Many times you will have to do something you don't feel like doing. Like washing dishes, for instance. Or doing homework. Or babysitting your kid brother. Or plucking weeds out of the garden.

If anyone understood sacrifice, Esther did. When she made the decision to enter the king's throne room unannounced, she knew that he could very well have her put to death. (Yep. That's how it was back then!) But even though she thought the journey might end in the ultimate sacrifice (death), she was willing to go anyway. Why? To save her people.

Hopefully, you'll never face anything that big, but life will offer you plenty of opportunities to give of yourself sacrificially. Whether it's giving up your plans so that someone else in the family can see their plans come to pass or saying no to a friend so you can visit your grandparents, these decisions will always result in joy in the end.

So don't look at *sacrifice* as a bad word. It's definitely not.

I will humble myself and live a sacrificial life, Lord!
I will pour out myself for others. Amen.

SIMPLE SACRIFICES

*And do not forget to do good and to share with
others, for with such sacrifices God is pleased.*
HEBREWS 13:16 NIV

Some people think that sacrificial living means you must go out of your
way to do really big, extravagant things for others. Maybe you've seen
this on TV, where a celebrity gives a big gift—say, a car—to someone.
These feel-good moments are fun, for sure. While you might occasionally
be asked to make big sacrifices, most sacrifices are small ones.

Waving at an elderly neighbor. Taking the trash out for her. Baking
cookies for a friend who is going through a hard time. Offering to do the
dishes for your sister while she studies for finals. These are the simple
sacrifices that will go a long, long way in endearing you to others.

And guess what? God is pleased with simple sacrifices too. He's not
asking you to climb mountains, girl. He might just be asking you to walk
next door and help a neighbor in need.

*I understand what You mean, Lord. Every little deed is a big
deed in Your eyes and in the eyes of others. I want to bless them
today by paying attention and helping where I can. Amen.*

A FRAGRANT OFFERING

*And walk in love, as Christ loved us and gave himself
up for us, a fragrant offering and sacrifice to God.*
EPHESIANS 5:2 ESV

Do you have a favorite perfume? When you find one you fall in love with, you want to wear it all the time!

God wants you to be a fragrant offering to those around you. The aroma of your life needs to be pleasing to others, just like that perfume. That means you must have a good attitude, a pleasant demeanor, a willing heart, and a desire to bless others and to (sometimes!) put their needs above your own.

This is really what it means to walk in love—to give as Jesus gave. He literally gave His all for us. What an amazing sacrifice! And we learn through this amazing offering how He wants us to live—always giving, always loving, always serving.

Demonstrate your love for Him by showing love to others. It's really that simple. Give off a lovely aroma, girl!

*I will remind myself, every time I put on perfume, that
You want me to be a fragrant offering to others, Lord.
May they see my kindness and be won to You. Amen.*

A SET-APART TIME

Then Esther told them to reply to Mordecai, "Go, gather all the Jews to be found in Susa, and hold a fast on my behalf, and do not eat or drink for three days, night or day. I and my young women will also fast as you do. Then I will go to the king, though it is against the law, and if I perish, I perish."

ESTHER 4:15–16 ESV

. . . .

No one ever said life was going to be easy. You'll go through lots of things that aren't fair. Others will get attention that you deserve. People will be elevated, and you'll be left behind. These things happen in life, and they don't make sense to you.

Esther understood what it felt like to struggle. When she realized the dire condition her people were in, she asked Mordecai to gather them together to fast for three days and nights. She agreed to do the same.

Her motive? If they all struggled together through the fast, pleading with God for mercy, maybe He would spare her life when she faced the king. (Spoiler alert: the king not only spared her life but listened and believed.)

Look at her last words: "If I perish, I perish." Esther was a woman who was willing to lay everything—literally everything—on the line for her people.

Life is hard sometimes, Jesus, but like Esther I want to give my all. Help me even when it's difficult. Amen.

FOR GOD SO LOVED, HE GAVE

For God so loved the world that he gave his one
and only Son, that whoever believes in him
shall not perish but have eternal life.
JOHN 3:16 NIV

John 3:16 is the most popular verse in the Bible, and it's easy to see why. In this one simple verse, we learn everything we need to know about our Father God. He loves us so much that He was willing to give the one thing that was more important to Him than anything, His Son.

He asks for only one thing in return, and it's a very important thing. He wants your heart. When you place your trust in Christ—when you say, "Come and take my heart, Jesus. Come and live inside me and be the King of my life"—you're validating His gift.

Think about it. If you gave an expensive gift to your mom and she never opened it or used it, how would that make you feel? That's a little like how God must feel when people refuse to accept the gift that Jesus gave on the cross.

It takes courage to start your life over as a new creation in Christ, but guess what? From that moment on, the God of the universe will never leave you! He loves you that much, girl.

Thank You for dying for me, Jesus. I accept that gift!
With the power of Your Holy Spirit in me, I won't
break Your heart. I'll live for You all my life. Amen.

A LIVING SACRIFICE

So then, my friends, because of God's great mercy to us
I appeal to you: Offer yourselves as a living sacrifice
to God, dedicated to his service and pleasing to him.
This is the true worship that you should offer.
ROMANS 12:1 GNT

. . . .

In the Old Testament, the priest would offer yearly sacrifices to the Lord for the forgiveness of the sins of the people. He would slaughter on an altar the unblemished (perfect) animals the people would bring to him as offerings. The animals' blood was the sacrifice.

When Jesus died, God put an end to animal sacrifices. What Jesus did was more than enough. And here's the best part. Like those animals He really did die, but Jesus did something none of those beasts ever could: He rose from the grave!

You'll never have to offer your life as Jesus did. Any sacrifices you make in this lifetime will be living sacrifices. Doing good things for others. Going out of your way to make a difference. It takes courage to live sacrificially, but what a blessed way to live!

I will be a living sacrifice, Jesus. I'll offer myself—wholly and
completely—to Your service and Your kingdom. Amen.

A SACRIFICE OF PRAISE

Through Jesus, therefore, let us continually offer to God a sacrifice of praise—the fruit of lips that openly profess his name.
HEBREWS 13:15 NIV

• •

Have you ever had a day when you just weren't feeling it? Maybe you woke up in a bad mood and the day only went downhill from there.

On those days, there's one very important thing you can do to turn things around in a hurry, and it might surprise you. Offer God the sacrifice of praise!

Turn on some praise and worship music and begin to sing, girl! Give yourself over to the words, the melody, and the heart of the songs. Let them wash over you, and then watch as God begins to make your day better.

God wants you to continually offer a sacrifice of praise (even on the days when you don't feel like it). Why? Because He knows that healing comes during your intimate times with Him, and oftentimes turning your heart to praise and worship will lead you into an intimate time.

In that holy place, let go of your frustrations. Let go of your anger. Let go of your pain. With your lips, sing out nothing but praises in their place.

*I will praise You with my mouth, Jesus. I'll offer
a sacrifice of praise even on the hardest of days.
I'm trusting You to turn things around! Amen.*

A SPIRITUAL HOUSE

Come as living stones, and let yourselves be used in building the spiritual temple, where you will serve as holy priests to offer spiritual and acceptable sacrifices to God through Jesus Christ.

1 PETER 2:5 GNT

When a mason prepares to build a house out of stone, he examines those stones in advance to see how and where they will fit together. Stone by stone, the house is built with mortar (similar to concrete) between them, holding them in place.

God is building a spiritual house, and He's using you as part of the process. He wants you to serve as a holy priest in that house He's building.

Remember those Old Testament priests we talked about before? Well, now God is saying, "You are one of them." Thank goodness you don't have to slaughter any bulls. (That would be awkward!) But He's asking you to offer spiritual and acceptable sacrifices.

"Spiritual" means you've prayed it through. You're not just randomly showing up with something to offer. You've come with a plan. "Acceptable" means you're offering something that will make God's heart happy.

Let Him shape you into a spiritual house so that you're ready to offer spiritual and acceptable sacrifices that will please the heart of your Father God.

I will come, willing and ready to offer all I am to You, Jesus. Amen.

EVERYTHING PALES IN COMPARISON

*But whatever gain I had, I counted
as loss for the sake of Christ.*
PHILIPPIANS 3:7 ESV

Imagine you wanted to enter a beauty contest. You found the perfect ball gown for the finale, practiced your skills for the talent portion, and prepared yourself for the Q&A part. In short, you went fully prepped. Nervous but prepped.

Now imagine you won that competition. Your hard work paid off. The roar of applause might just go to your head, right? And that dazzling crown they placed on your head afterward? Wow! Talk about feeling special.

What would it feel like if you got all the applause in the world but never came to know Christ? As this verse says, you would count it all as loss. Nothing in this world—not even the most prestigious awards—will even come close to knowing and loving Him. No matter what gain you have, it pales in comparison to what Jesus can offer.

*Everything pales in comparison to You, Lord! The things of
this world are fun and enjoyable, but even the very best things
don't even come close to knowing You! Thanks for the reminder
that You are the best of the best, my everything! Amen.*

FOR HIS SAKE

"For whoever would save his life will lose it,
but whoever loses his life for my sake will save it."
LUKE 9:24 ESV

Throughout history many believers have been persecuted and martyred for their faith in Jesus. They paid the ultimate price.

Did you realize that most of Jesus' disciples died agonizing deaths, even being crucified upside down? It's true. They were willing to pay that price because of their deep, abiding faith in Jesus. And even in the very midst of the agony, many forgave the ones harming them.

Consider all this in light of today's verse. Those who gave their lives for the sake of the gospel will be saved. Those martyrs realized the truth, that momentary pain would send them directly into the arms of Jesus.

Even now there are people around the globe who are courageously facing their accusers as they refuse to denounce their faith. Many are being put to death. As you go about your daily life, as you think about how hard your life is, compare it to those who are paying the ultimate price. Perspective is everything, isn't it?

Lord, please be with those believers who are facing
persecution around the world. May we never
forget their courage and their faith. Amen.

BE OF THE SAME MIND

*Complete my joy by being of the same mind, having the
same love, being in full accord and of one mind.*
PHILIPPIANS 2:2 ESV

Have you ever heard the expression "There's power in numbers"? It's true! When you have to face an enemy, for instance, you always feel more secure if you're surrounded by like-minded people.

Esther was connected to people of like faith. They understood each other. It's great to be with people who "get" you, isn't it?

Because Esther had the support of other believers, she had a prayer team when it was time to face the king. The prayers of her people made her strong and courageous. And she came out of that experience braver and more courageous because of their prayers.

Now think about your life. Who do you know of like faith? Who would you go to if you needed someone to pray for you in a tough situation? It's important to have these people in your life, and it's also critical to be that person for others.

We need each other. That's the long and short of it. Working in unity with others of similar faith will make you stronger, inside and out.

Thank You for surrounding me with people who can lift me up and pray for me, Lord. Show me how I can be that person for others. Amen.

RELIABLE SOURCES

*Take the teachings that you heard me proclaim in
the presence of many witnesses, and entrust them to
reliable people, who will be able to teach others also.*
2 Timothy 2:2 gnt

. . . .

Would you say that you know a lot of reliable people? How many in your inner circle follow through and do what they say they're going to do? Now examine your outer circle.

There's a reason the Bible tells us to take God's teaching to reliable sources. They will take that word and run with it. (Let's face it—not everyone is genuinely interested in being transformed. Most just want to feel better.)

Does this mean you shouldn't share God's teachings with unreliable people? Absolutely not! But if you're entrusting God's teachings to people, let it be to the reliable ones. Why? So that they can, in turn, share that good news with others.

Now, think again. Which reliable, trustworthy friends would you choose to share your testimony, your goals, and your dreams with? Who will build you up and not encourage you to take a different, easier path? It might take courage to open up and share what God is doing (and what you hope to see Him do), but find a reliable friend and share to your heart's content.

*Show me who is trustworthy, Lord! I will proclaim the
truth, especially to the ones who can be trusted. Amen.*

UNITY OF MIND

Finally, all of you, have unity of mind, sympathy,
brotherly love, a tender heart, and a humble mind.
1 PETER 3:8 ESV

- -

Esther had to change her mindset from queen to young Jewish girl. The Jews were like-minded in their beliefs, their actions, and how they lived.

When she changed her thinking to be in unity with her people, Esther's courage rose. For them she could do anything—even bravely face the king to make a request on their behalf.

Who do you walk in unity with? Do you have friends, family members, or fellow students who are like-minded? You feel stronger when you're with these people.

Maybe you're part of an after-school (or before-school) student-led prayer group. Maybe you're in FCA (Fellowship of Christian Athletes). Even if you're not part of an official organization, you can grow stronger in your faith by spending time with people who have the same belief system as you. That way, when you're tempted to do the wrong thing, you'll have someone to go to who can encourage you to keep walking the right path.

Unity is a very good thing. God feels very strongly about it, especially with His kids! So stick together.

I don't want to get off on my own, Lord. I want to
walk in unity with other people who believe like me.
Show me who I can stand strong with. Amen.

WE'RE ALL PART OF THE SAME BODY

For just as the body is one and has many members,
and all the members of the body, though many,
are one body, so it is with Christ.
1 CORINTHIANS 12:12 ESV

Isn't it fascinating to think about how God created the human body? He gave you two hands, two feet, two eyes, two ears. He gave you a mouth to speak with and skin, bones, and muscles to protect your internal organs.

Now imagine if you suddenly lost the use of one arm. Or one foot. Or one eye. What if you lost your hearing or the ability to speak? Without the use of just that one thing, everything else has to work harder. (Side note: You've probably heard this already, but blind people have very keen senses, which helps them make up for the lack of vision. The same is true with deaf people. Their vision is sharp, as they read lips and watch for signs of what's being said.)

Here's the point: Every part of the body is important. And the same is true in the body of Christ. If one person is weak or ineffective, it affects everyone. This is one more reason why you have to be brave and speak up when you're around your friends. They are counting on you to be strong. Together believers are a force to be reckoned with!

Lord, I have a role to play, and I want to
be the strongest I can be in You. Amen.

BREAKING DOWN THE WALLS

*For Christ himself has brought us peace by making Jews
and Gentiles one people. With his own body he broke down
the wall that separated them and kept them enemies.*
EPHESIANS 2:14 GNT

. . . .

Have you ever felt like an invisible wall has gone up between you and a friend? It's weird, isn't it? It's a transparent wall, but there's been an odd separation that makes you feel uncomfortable whenever she's around.

This is how the enemy works, by the way. He wants to put up walls between you and the very people God has intended to be in your life. Why? Because he knows you will grow stronger in your faith as your relationships with godly friends increase. So be aware of the enemy's tactics.

Now think about your relationship with God. Sometimes walls go up, even in your relationship with Him. He wants every wall to come down—the ones separating you from your mentors and friends and the ones you've built around your heart to keep Him out. Today, acknowledge those walls. Then speak to them in the name of Jesus. They must come down at the mention of His name!

*In Your name, Jesus, I speak to the walls in my life!
Please put an end to any division between myself and
godly friends. And strengthen my relationship with You
as walls around my heart come down too. Amen.*

WORK YOUR WAY TOWARD PEACE

*Let us therefore make every effort to do what
leads to peace and to mutual edification.*
ROMANS 14:19 NIV

· ·

It's kind of weird to think that peace requires effort, but it does. Think about the different countries around the world. They all have different customs, different beliefs, different political systems. And yet they try their best to get along.

Sometimes it doesn't go so well, and countries end up at war. Then chaos ensues.

Yes, peace certainly requires effort, and that's true in relationships too. There's a big difference between being a peacekeeper (doing or saying things to keep the peace) and being a peacemaker (doing the hard work to make the relationship work). God wants you to be a peacemaker. It won't be easy. You might have to speak truth to a friend who has fallen away from God or confess some things to your parents that you've been withholding.

Once you finally do that hard work, true peace comes. Anything that falls short of true peace is only temporary anyway. It's an illusion. You want the real deal. Walking in peace will affect every single area of your life. So be brave! Be a peacemaker today.

*I get it, Jesus. This peacemaking thing won't be easy. But I'll do the
hard work so I have true peace in every area of my life. Amen.*

DIFFERENT GIFTS

*For as in one body we have many members, and the
members do not all have the same function.*
ROMANS 12:4 ESV

We talked about hands, feet, ears, and eyes earlier, but here's something to think about: Do all those "members" of your body do the same thing? Do your feet do the work of your ears? Do your eyes do the work of your tongue? Do your fingers do the work of your heart?

Absolutely not! Each member of the body serves its purpose, and each purpose is completely unique. But they all work together! The heart beats and causes the fingers to be able to move.

You get the idea. The same is true in the body of Christ. Look around you the next time you're at church. The people don't look the same, dress the same, or have the same talents or abilities. And yet every single person is a member of the body. And when they work together, things get done!

Don't discount some other member's gifts or talents just because they're different from yours. And for that matter, don't be hard on yourself either. You fit in, in your own unique way. The body just wouldn't be the same without you!

*I don't mind being unique, Jesus! I'll use the gifts
You gave me to work with others so that we can
accomplish great things for You. Amen.*

YOU FIT

See what kind of love the Father has given to us, that we should be called children of God; and so we are. The reason why the world does not know us is that it did not know him.

1 JOHN 3:1 ESV

Do you ever feel like people just don't get you? They don't understand your quirks or your way of doing things. Take a close look at the verse above and you'll see the reason for this: "The reason why the world does not know us is that it did not know him."

You're different because, well, you're different. You're a child of God, part of the heavenly kingdom. The world doesn't understand that you've stepped into the light and they're still walking in darkness. They expect you to act like them, and it seems weird if you don't.

Oh, but the joy of living in the light makes it all worth it! "See what kind of love the Father has given to us"! (Doesn't that get you excited?) You're His kid. He calls you His child, and so you are. You never have to question where you fit in or whose you are. You're His—totally and completely.

So don't spend a lot of time fretting over fitting in with the world, girl. You weren't meant to. You were made to stand out!

I'll stop worrying about fitting in, Jesus! I am so excited to be part of Your family. The only opinion that matters is Yours. Amen.

PARTING WORDS

And now, my friends, good-bye! Strive for perfection;
listen to my appeals; agree with one another; live in peace.
And the God of love and peace will be with you.
2 Corinthians 13:11 gnt

Back in biblical times, the city of Corinth was a commercial area with an international reputation. Christians were in the minority in this city, and many of them were young in their faith. The apostle Paul discipled them and, after leaving them to travel elsewhere, sent letters to encourage them.

In these letters, Paul gave them all sorts of great advice for how to live, but one thing he stressed: live in unity. He asked them to strive for perfection in this area. He wanted them to learn how to agree with one another and to live in peace.

Those words are just as powerful today, and you could easily write them in a letter to your friends who are new to the faith: do your best to get along and be unified.

Why? Because there's power in unity. Divided we fall. Together we conquer. So don't let little squabbles tear you apart from the Christians you know. Strive for perfection in this. Live in unity.

I will do my best not to let problems tear me away from other believers, Jesus, but I will need Your help, for sure! Amen.

PUT ON LOVE

*And above all these put on love, which binds
everything together in perfect harmony.*
COLOSSIANS 3:14 ESV

Many times in the Word of God we're told that love is the most important thing. Sometimes it takes courage to show love to someone, especially if they have hurt you in the past. Of course this doesn't mean you put yourself in harm's way or allow yourself to be taken advantage of. That's not God's will for you.

Why does the Lord care so much about love? Because it's the thread that binds everything else together. When you're faced with enemies, love. When you're faced with people who believe differently, love.

You have to dress yourself in love every single day in order to face any opposition that comes your way. Slip it on like a pair of jeans or your favorite T-shirt. Wear it all day long when you're up against even the toughest of people.

Love conquers all.

*I will put on love, Jesus. It won't be easy, especially not with
some of the people I know. But You promise success when
I let love lead the way, so that's what I'll do. Amen.*

YOU HAVE BEEN STRATEGICALLY PLACED

*Whatever you do, work heartily, as for the Lord and not
for men, knowing that from the Lord you will receive the
inheritance as your reward. You are serving the Lord Christ.*
COLOSSIANS 3:23–24 ESV

Esther wasn't born just for such a *time* as this; she was born for such a *place* as this too. God put her in the palace with the king so that she could perform the duties He had laid out for her.

God has strategically placed you too. He didn't just randomly pick your house, your neighborhood, your school, or your job. A heavenly strategy has been at play in all of that.

Knowing that you've been placed should change your entire perspective. Instead of asking the "Why am I here?" question, replace it with "What can I do while I'm here? What plans do You have for me, God?"

Queen Esther asked those questions, and God ended up using her to save an entire people group! He has great plans for you too. So stop kicking. Stop fighting. Settle into the place He has you, and start to think of ways you can impact that place for the kingdom of God!

*I'll stop fighting it, God. I won't argue with You about where
You've put me. Instead, I'll look for creative ways to do more
in this place. I'll move with godly strategy. Thank You for
the reminder that where I am is no accident. Amen.*

GET SALTY, GIRL!

"You are the salt of the earth, but if salt has lost its taste, how shall its saltiness be restored? It is no longer good for anything except to be thrown out and trampled under people's feet. You are the light of the world. A city set on a hill cannot be hidden."
MATTHEW 5:13–14 ESV

Imagine you're in a restaurant and about to eat a juicy steak. You take a bite, and it's a little bland. Not what you expected, especially at the price you're paying for it. (Hey, steak isn't cheap!)

You reach for the saltshaker and sprinkle some on, but it doesn't seem to change the flavor at all. So you sprinkle a little more. Weird. The salt seems to have lost its saltiness.

That might seem like a silly example, but in this biblical illustration, you are the salt. God put you on the table (planet Earth) to be salty (not in the twenty-first-century interpretation but in a "flavorful" way). He has put you here to change the bland, boring lives of people around you.

You're the salt of the earth. Be bold with that flavor, girl! Don't try to hide who you are or what you believe. What good would that do? You would be like that shaker, filled with nothing but air.

Don't be air. Be salt. Real, genuine, salty salt.

Lord, sometimes it's easier to pretend I'm not a Christian. But when I do that, I don't impact anyone. I want to make a difference, Jesus, so help me maintain my saltiness no matter how difficult. Amen.

TRUST GOD IN THE WAITING

There is a time for everything, and a season
for every activity under the heavens.
ECCLESIASTES 3:1 NIV

Sometimes one of the most courageous things you can do is wait. Maybe you've prayed for something specific. You feel very strongly about it, and you're hoping God will come through for you. But so far nothing has happened to bring any hope that He will.

Remember, God's Word says there's a time for everything. Of course, not every prayer request will be granted as you expect. God is not a genie in a bottle. But if you've prayed for something that's in His will for you, it could just be that it's a matter of waiting for His perfect timing.

You never want to get ahead of God. That can be very dangerous. Some people force things to happen and then live to regret it later. Stay patient. Stay calm. Trust God in the waiting. Then, when that big moment finally arrives, think of how amazing you're going to feel!

In His time, girl. In His time.

I'll wait on You, Jesus. I won't rush ahead or demand things
on my schedule. I know Your thoughts are higher than my
thoughts and Your ways are higher than my ways. I'll trust
You in the waiting. Give me courage, I pray. Amen.

GOING OUT AND COMING IN

*The Lord will keep your going out and your
coming in from this time forth and forevermore.*
PSALM 121:8 ESV

Think about it: if God can keep your going out and your coming in from today until eternity, surely He must know where you're headed.

You don't, of course. Not having any clue where the road will take you can be scary. But you can trust in the one who created you. He knows every single minute of every single day where you will be, who you'll be with, and what you'll be doing.

That should bring you tremendous peace, girl!

And remember this: When you walk out the door of your house to head to school or work or to visit a friend, God goes with you. And when you walk back in again, He'll be with you then too.

No matter where you're going or what time of day or night, the Lord has you covered. What an amazing God we serve!

*Thank You for taking such great care of me, God. You know
exactly where I'm headed, and You're looking out for me
every step of the way. I am so grateful I can trust You. Amen.*

HE'S GOING WITH YOU

*If I flew away beyond the east or lived in the
farthest place in the west, you would be there
to lead me, you would be there to help me.*
PSALM 139:9–10 GNT

Some families are separated by distance. Maybe you have an older sibling who has moved away or a grandparent who lives in another state or even another country. Keeping the family together with so much distance between members can be difficult.

When a child moves away to a different state, the parents have no idea what the child's up to. But that's not true with God and His kids. No matter which state you move to, He is going with you. Headed to Michigan? He'll be with you. Going to California? He'll be there as well! Headed off on a mission trip to Managua, Nicaragua? God has His bags all packed because He's coming with you!

No matter where you fly, little birdie, you won't be alone. Your heavenly Father isn't just settled into the airplane seat next to you; He's leading the way. (He's the one who gave you that idea to go on that mission trip!)

You don't have to be afraid, no matter where you're headed. You'll never be alone.

*You're the best traveling companion ever, God!
I'm grateful to have You leading the way. Amen.*

GOD'S STRATEGY

For by him all things were created, in heaven and on earth,
visible and invisible, whether thrones or dominions or rulers or
authorities—all things were created through him and for him.
COLOSSIANS 1:16 ESV

It stands to reason that the Creator of everything would know the intimate details of all those things. He knows the rivers and the seas. He understands the weather and the planets. He has a handle on the animals and the fish in the ocean. He even knew you before you were born.

There's literally nothing you can point to that God doesn't understand. He can even see into the spiritual realm to know the battles going on there.

If He knows it all, then you can trust that He has carefully strategized it all. He knows where you're going to be at any given time, but He also knows who else is going to be there with you—both good and bad. He knows the situations you have faced and the ones you have yet to face. And He has already strategized ways to see you through them.

God loves you. He will only place you where you will grow and flourish. So don't be afraid. Be courageous as you step ahead.

I trust You even when I don't know where I'm going or what I'm
doing, Lord. You know, and that's all that matters! Amen.

COUNT THE COST

"If one of you is planning to build a tower, you sit down first and figure out what it will cost, to see if you have enough money to finish the job."
LUKE 14:28 GNT

• •

There's so much truth in today's verse! If you set out to build something big—a house, a tower, a vacation home—you would count the cost ahead of making your decision. You wouldn't want to get in over your head, after all!

The same is true when you buy that first car or rent that first apartment. You have to take a look at your finances to see what's reasonable. Otherwise you'll be drowning in debt, and that's no fun!

There are a lot of things to be built ahead—friendships, jobs, college, and romantic relationships. Before you dive headfirst into any of that, count the cost. Don't make crazy, impulsive decisions you'll regret later, girl. Moving with such caution when others around you are rushing ahead will take courage, but you need to be wise. Count the cost.

I get it, Jesus. I don't want to have regrets later. I'll count the cost before I make big decisions so that I don't end up in trouble later on! Thanks for always guiding me! Amen.

YOUR PLANS OR HIS?

In their hearts humans plan their course,
but the LORD establishes their steps.
PROVERBS 16:9 NIV

Making plans is fun, isn't it? Maybe you're one of those girls who knows exactly what she wants to be when she grows up. You know what college you'll attend, what you'll study, what degree you'll get, and where you'll work when you're done. Or so you think. Sometimes plans don't exactly come to fruition the way you think they will!

Go ahead and make those plans. Have fun! Dream big! But be flexible, because you never know when life might just interrupt those plans and God will ask you to go His way instead of your own.

Some people aren't flexible at all. But being flexible was one of Esther's strongest attributes! She was flexible when it came to becoming queen and flexible once again when she was needed to take a stand for her people.

Flexible people accomplish great things, and there's no doubt you're going to as well. So brace yourself. The path ahead might not be perfectly straight, but it's going to be a lot of fun!

I will be flexible, Jesus. I won't be so stuck in my ways that
I refuse to bend. If You change my path, I'll gladly follow
You. I want to go where You want me to go. Amen.

A HOUSE IS BUILT BY WISDOM

*By wisdom a house is built, and through understanding
it is established; through knowledge its rooms are
filled with rare and beautiful treasures.*
PROVERBS 24:3–4 NIV

King Solomon built many amazing properties during his lifetime. He constructed the temple in Jerusalem, which turned out to be one of the most remarkable buildings of its time. He also built his own palace, as well as lots of other things, such as roads.

Solomon was a guy who knew a little something about building stuff! So keep that in mind as you read today's scripture. Buildings are constructed out of materials like stone, concrete, wood, steel, bricks, and so on. And many of today's modern homes are beyond beautiful! Some are even smart homes with all sorts of modern technology built in.

But what would be the point of building an amazing home if the people who lived inside of it didn't act wisely? What if they trashed the place? What if they fought and argued all the time? What if they did things that dishonored God and one another?

What makes a home lovely isn't just its physical decor but the lovely hearts of the people who dwell there. It takes time—and courage—to build a spiritual house, but you have it in you, girl!

*I get it, Jesus—You want to see me built up on the inside, a girl who
is wise beyond her years. With Your help, I will do my best. Amen.*

HE'S HERE

Jesus spoke to them at once. "Courage!"
he said. "It is I. Don't be afraid!"
MATTHEW 14:27 GNT

• •

It's easy to get spooked when you're in an unsettling situation. Maybe you just got your license and you're driving alone for the first time. Or maybe it's the first day of the school year in a new school and you don't know anyone.

You will have a million opportunities to feel frightened and overwhelmed in this life. But you will have just as many opportunities for Jesus to show up in a supernatural way and positively overwhelm you with His presence and reassurance.

Suddenly, there He is. He cries out, "Courage, sweet girl! It's Me. I'm here." And instantly, peace envelops you like a warm blanket on a chilly day. Everything is immediately all right.

When Jesus walks into a situation, nothing else matters. Let the wind blow. Let the storms rage. Let the people shout and roar. Jesus is here, and He has everything under control.

I'm so glad You keep showing up in my situations, Lord!
Sometimes I get myself into some tricky and hard places.
I'm grateful for Your presence and Your comfort. Amen.

HE WILL DELIVER YOU

"I wait for your deliverance, LORD."
GENESIS 49:18 GNT

. . . .

Do you believe that God can—and will—deliver you? When you're at the bottom of a well, when all of life's circumstances seem to be coming against you, can you peek up at a glimmer of sunlight and imagine that things will somehow get better?

Not every situation ends the way you hope, but try to have the faith of Esther even on hard days. God was her deliverer, and He is your deliverer too. That's not to say He'll miraculously lift you out of the hard stuff right away, but "deliverance" often means He will give you internal freedom even when outward circumstances are still hard.

In other words, God will give you the ability to supernaturally rise above what you're going through. So don't give up. Don't give in to depression or feelings of despair. Your deliverer is right there next to you no matter what the circumstances look like.

*Thank You, Lord, my great deliverer! You set me free—
from anxiety, frustration, and feelings of hopelessness.
I will follow You, and I won't give up no matter what
the external circumstances look like. Amen.*

RANDOM FAILURES

*"Be determined and confident. Do not be afraid
of them. Your God, the LORD himself, will be with
you. He will not fail you or abandon you."*
DEUTERONOMY 31:6 GNT

Even the very best student occasionally has an off day. If you're one of those girls who strives to get an A on every test, a 100 on every project, and a 4.0 GPA, you probably work extra hard to make sure you find success.

But let's face it—everyone fails from time to time. Even a straight A student will occasionally make a B or a C.

Think about a family that has just adopted a puppy. She's an adorable little thing, and she tries hard to please you. She sits, stays, and mostly does her business in the yard, not the house. Do you get mad at her when she chews up the toilet paper roll or pees on the rug? Okay, maybe you get a little upset, but you get the idea: you're not getting rid of her because of a few rough moments.

Now think about God. Does He ever have an off day? Does He make random mistakes? Absolutely not! Humans will fail from time to time, but your awesome heavenly Father will never fail you no matter what.

*I'm so glad You don't make mistakes, Lord. I can trust
You to do the right thing every time. I won't be afraid
as long as You're in charge of my life. Amen.*

WHEN IN DOUBT, PRAY

I prayed to the Lord, and he answered me;
he freed me from all my fears.
Psalm 34:4 gnt

. . . .

Can you imagine how your parents would feel if you went through a weird phase and refused to communicate with them? No doubt they would be hurt, confused, and maybe even a little upset.

Now imagine how God must feel when He watches you, His child, struggle with fear and pain without reaching out to Him. How many times a day does He stretch His arms in your direction and say, "I'm right here! Come to Me!"

You're busy. All girls are. You have places to be and things to do. No one blames you for that. But when you're going through something, don't forget to reach out to God. If you don't pray, you might be limiting His intervention. Don't believe that? Read today's verse: "I prayed. . .he answered." How can He answer when you don't ask?

What are you facing today? Instead of tackling it on your own, instead of running to a friend with your problem, go to Jesus. He longs to free you from your fears, and He's standing right there, waiting.

I won't keep You waiting, Jesus! I'll run
to You next time, I promise! Amen.

MOUNTAINS AND MIRACLES

"But you will receive power when the Holy Spirit has come upon you, and you will be my witnesses in Jerusalem and in all Judea and Samaria, and to the end of the earth."

ACTS 1:8 ESV

The power of the Holy Spirit gives us courage and delivers us from fear even when we're in the middle of a terrible battle or a life-changing storm. The Spirit of God is more than just a comforter. He offers discernment, protection, and (above all) power to work miracles.

When you read that, what comes to mind? What sort of miracles are you believing God for today? Are you facing a mountain so big that you wonder if it can move at all? He created the universe! With just a word, He spoke worlds into existence. Animals breathe because of Him. Rivers flow because of Him. You exist because of Him!

God is still working miracles today, so what are you waiting for? You can speak to the mountains in your life, girl. With the Holy Spirit residing inside of you, you can move in power and courage no matter what you're facing.

Today I speak to the mountain of fear that has risen up in my life, Lord! In Your name it has to come crashing down. Amen.

A SAFE SHELTER

*You hide them in the safety of your presence from
the plots of others; in a safe shelter you hide
them from the insults of their enemies.*
PSALM 31:20 GNT

• •

Have you ever been through a terrible storm? If you live along the coast, perhaps you've faced hurricane-force winds. They can be terrifying as they roar past your house, shaking everything in their way and knocking down trees and power lines.

In the middle of a storm, you need to get yourself to a safe space. An enclosed bathroom. A closet. A basement.

The same is true when you go through emotional or psychological storms, including broken friendships, false accusations, or extreme peer pressure. You need a safe space to hide away until things calm down. Thank goodness for the Lord! Take a close look at this verse and you'll see that God is with you in the storm. He has a safe shelter just for you.

Spend time hiding away with Jesus when you're in the throes of an emotional hurricane and you'll see that He meets you there. In that quiet, peaceful place, He can offer direction and bring a sense of calm no matter how rough the winds.

*I won't run into the storm, Jesus. I will run to You instead. Thank
You for offering shelter during rough seasons when people are out
to get me. I know I can trust You, so I choose to be with You. Amen.*

A WARM BLANKET

"Peace is what I leave with you; it is my own peace
that I give you. I do not give it as the world does.
Do not be worried and upset; do not be afraid."
JOHN 14:27 GNT

Imagine you were super stressed out, so you scheduled an appointment with a therapist. She helped you talk through your troubles then gave you some deep-breathing exercises to do at home.

Those exercises would help in the middle of a stressful moment, but long-lasting peace would be a little more elusive. Therapy would help, of course. It's always a good idea to talk out your problems, but God's peace goes beyond even the best therapy.

God's peace is matchless, for it can surround you like a warm blanket even in the very middle of a crisis. You often hear people who've been in terrible accidents say things like "It's like God was right there in the car with me."

God's peace is like a river washing over you. And it's available anytime you call out to Him. The Holy Spirit, your comforter, is also a peace giver. So don't wait until you're in a crisis. Right now, before things get rough, allow that river to sweep over you and bring true and lasting peace.

I need God-breathed peace, Lord! I don't want a quick fix. I have
so many stressors in my life. I need a river of peace! Today I say,
"Please come and wash over me with life-changing peace!" Amen.

TRUSTING GOD FOR BIG THINGS

"For nothing will be impossible with God."
LUKE 1:37 ESV

· ·

When you hear the phrase "human limits," what comes to mind? What are a few things humans can't do that only God can?

Here's a quick list to consider: humans can't heal, create life, make rivers flow, cause mountains to tumble.

Now, you're probably thinking, *Yes, they can! Doctors heal all the time. And moms and dads create tiny human lives. Dams can cause rivers to flow in whatever direction they're instructed, and mountains can tumble if dynamite is used.*

There's a problem with your theory though. Everything humans make or do starts with something that God made or did. Doctors heal through medicines, but God created everything necessary to make those meds. Moms and dads have babies, but that child is being born out of another human life. (And remember, all human life began with Adam and Eve.) Rivers can be redirected, but humans can't instruct the water to flow a certain way, as God can. And dynamite can tumble mountains, but God created the chemicals necessary to create dynamite.

You get the idea. Humans are limited, but nothing is impossible with God. When you're reminded of that, are you emboldened to believe for big things? Today, put your faith in the miraculous power of a God who can perform miracles!

I'm trusting You for big things today, Jesus! Amen.

THE WEAPONS WE FIGHT WITH

*The weapons we fight with are not the weapons
of the world. On the contrary, they have divine
power to demolish strongholds.*
2 Corinthians 10:4 niv

Imagine that a warrior headed off to battle with no weapons. Talk about feeling vulnerable! He would step out onto the battlefield, bullets and missiles whizzing around him, completely unable to defend himself.

God has given you weapons that are even better than physical ones. The battle you're fighting is taking place in the spiritual realm, and the Lord has given you spiritual weapons to fight it. He has given you a helmet of salvation, a breastplate of righteousness, a belt of truth, shoes of peace, and the sword of the Spirit. God has also given you a shield of faith that you can raise every time the enemy tries to fire off those nasty arrows of doubt, insecurity, and pain.

Above those things, you've been given the power to pray, to fast, and to speak boldly against any opposition that comes your way. So don't go looking for physical weapons, girl. You won't need them. What you already have inside of you is more than enough.

*I will use Your weapons to defend myself against the
fiery darts of the enemy, Lord. I won't look to myself
for answers. I will courageously lean on You. Amen.*

GOD'S HIDING PLACE

Whoever dwells in the shelter of the Most High will rest in the shadow of the Almighty. I will say of the LORD, "He is my refuge and my fortress, my God, in whom I trust."
PSALM 91:1–2 NIV

Remember how you used to play hide-and-seek when you were little? Hiding away in the closet was always a bit scary, but you pretty much knew you were going to be discovered. Still, you did your best to find the safest hiding spot so that you wouldn't be located too easily.

When you're going through a stressful season and you're feeling afraid, there's a hiding place you can run to where you'll be completely safe. Your hands won't tremble. Your knees won't shake. You won't be looking over your shoulder, wondering if the enemy is about to sneak up on you.

In God's hiding place, He tucks you away for a time of relief from the world. And the best part is that you can run to this place anytime of the day or night. He will meet you there and bring comfort and peace even if you're in great turmoil.

Don't run from. Run to. Run to Him, girl. He has you covered no matter how terrified you might be.

Thank You for that perfect hiding place, Jesus, because I have days when I need a shelter, a place to hide from the craziness. I'm so grateful I can trust in You. Amen.

AN ARMY OF ANGELS

If you say, "The LORD is my refuge," and you make the Most High
your dwelling, no harm will overtake you, no disaster will come
near your tent. For he will command his angels concerning
you to guard you in all your ways; they will lift you up in their
hands, so that you will not strike your foot against a stone.
PSALM 91:9–12 NIV

Wow, talk about a huge promise from God! Basically, He calls together the team and says, "Cover this girl with your wings, guys. She's in a tough spot."

And they do! Those angels rush in around you and guard you in all your ways—not just in the hiding place but when you come back out to face all those troubles you've been so afraid of.

How does it make you feel to know there's an army of angels camped around you as you come up against the opposition? It should strengthen your faith, for sure!

Those same angels are going to lift you with their hands so you won't face injury even in the middle of the battle.

Wow! It's great to have God on your side!

I'm so glad You've sent Your angels to guard and protect
me, Jesus. Thank You for keeping me safe! Amen.

IN IT TO WIN IT

Do you not know that in a race all the runners run, but only one gets the prize? Run in such a way as to get the prize.
1 CORINTHIANS 9:24 NIV

Imagine you're a baseball player and the game is in the final inning. Your team is down by five points. It seems impossible. The clock is ticking, and the game will be over soon.

It's your turn at bat. You're not feeling terribly confident, and you can't imagine how you could possibly turn this situation around.

Can you see, just by your attitude, how your outcome might be impacted by negative thinking? If you're sure you won't, you won't. If you think you can, you might.

God wants you to think you can. He wants you, like Esther, to believe for the things that seem impossible. This includes big things and small things.

Don't give up hope even when others around you seem to be doing so. Keep smiling. Keep believing. Keep marching toward the goal even after others have dropped out of the race. They're watching you, girl. Give them hope.

I won't give in to negative thinking, Jesus! I'll keep my hope alive. I will keep on believing even when things seem impossible. You are a God of the impossible, after all! Amen.

SLOW AND STEADY WINS THE RACE

The plans of the diligent lead surely to abundance,
but everyone who is hasty comes only to poverty.
PROVERBS 21:5 ESV

Queen Esther was diligent. She didn't make fast, brash decisions. She carefully thought everything through.

Let's face it—most brash decisions come when you're panicked. You freak out and—*bam!*—you make a poor decision as a result.

The problem with human beings is that they want to fix everything, and usually in a hurry. But when you read today's verse, it's easy to see that slow and steady is God's way toward abundance. Those rash decisions and rushed projects? They're sloppy at best and risky at worst. It's fear that often leads people to make rushed and impulsive decisions. The next time fear comes over you and you feel the need to make everything all right in a hurry, stop and take a deep breath. Actually, take five or six deep breaths. Count to five as you inhale and five as you exhale. Calm yourself. Good decisions come on the heels of a peaceful mindset.

And remember, good things really come to those who wait. So don't be in such a hurry to fix everything, girl!

Okay, I'll slow down, Jesus! With Your help,
I'll stop making impulsive decisions. Amen.

DON'T BE EMBARRASSED TO HOPE

*And hope does not put us to shame, because God's
love has been poured into our hearts through
the Holy Spirit who has been given to us.*
ROMANS 5:5 ESV

· ·

Do you know someone who has given up hope? Maybe a friend with cancer or a neighbor whose marriage is on the rocks. Maybe you've even given up hope a few times yourself.

God says that hope does not disappoint us. In other words, you never have to feel ashamed for being hopeful. In some ways, hope is like a little candle flickering in the darkness. As long as it goes on flickering, you feel hopeful. But when that light goes away, fear sets in.

Hope keeps you from walking in fear. It's God's gift to you when you're going through a hard season. He pours out His love through the Holy Spirit, and when you sense that love, when you truly understand how much He adores and cherishes you, it gives you reason to hope again even if the circumstances don't look good.

No matter how your current situation looks at this very moment, don't give up hope. Keep that candle burning, girl. In doing so, you will encourage others who are going through hard times too.

*I won't give up hope, Lord. Thank You for loving
me so much and for keeping the flame lit! Amen.*

ALL THINGS

I can do all things through him who strengthens me.
PHILIPPIANS 4:13 ESV

. . . .

All things. Those two small words say a lot, don't they?

God's Word promises that you can do *all* things through Christ who gives you strength. The problem is you don't always call on Him, do you? If you're like most humans, you try to do things on your own. You figure out a plan and then implement it.

Finally, when nothing goes your way, you call on God for help. (Hey, it's basic human nature to want to fix things on your own, so you're not alone!)

God wants you to call on Him first. Before you ever set out to solve a problem or fix a broken relationship, ask for God's supernatural intervention. Then, after you've invited Him into the situation, trust that through Him you'll be strengthened to do anything and everything He asks you to do. It might not be easy. You might need extra courage. But with God leading the way (and you walking in direct obedience), you really will be able to conquer any situations you have to face.

I'll call on You first, Jesus. In my own strength, I can't get much done, but with You all things are possible. Thank You for that reminder today. Amen.

DON'T GET AHEAD OF GOD

*Guide me in your truth and teach me, for you are
God my Savior, and my hope is in you all day long.*
PSALM 25:5 NIV

• •

Sometimes you get really excited about things and dive in headfirst without much thought. You don't take the time to allow God to guide you. It's great to have enthusiasm, and it's wonderful to have hope, but be careful not to get ahead of God.

Queen Esther moved with great caution. She kept her hope alive, believing that God would spare her people. But she didn't dash into the throne room, jumping up and down, invigorated by hope. On the contrary, she moved slowly. Deliberately.

God wants you to move deliberately too. Life isn't a fifty-yard dash, girl. It's more like a marathon.

So keep running. Keep going. And when you make mistakes (and you surely will), learn from them. Let God pick you up, dust you off, and place you back on His path. Let Him guide you step-by-step toward each goal you will face in this life, without getting breathless along the way.

In other words, take your time. Slow down. Lean on God. Learn from Him.

*I won't be in a rush, Lord. I won't let my enthusiasm cause me
to behave impulsively. Instead, I'll take a deep breath and move
with the same deliberate caution that Esther did. Amen.*

YOUR INHERITANCE

*For those who are evil will be destroyed, but those
who hope in the LORD will inherit the land.*
PSALM 37:9 NIV

- -

Have you ever inherited anything? Maybe a grandmother passed away and left you a beautiful necklace. Or perhaps a distant relative or friend passed and left money to your family.

An inheritance is something that comes to you simply as a gift. It's not because of anything you did (or didn't do). It's just because of the close association that you receive the gift.

God gave you the best inheritance of all when He sent His Son, Jesus. You have inherited eternal life, girl! When things get crazy (as they often do), just take a deep breath and say, "It's okay. I'll get through this. I have an inheritance coming!"

Some people aren't in God's family, and they will never know the joy of eternal life with Him in heaven. They aren't going to inherit like you will. But they can if they come to know Him.

So swallow that fear and share the good news. Live in such a way that everyone ends up in the family!

*I want to lead others to You, Lord. Help me not
to be afraid as I share the good news. Amen.*

FLAWLESS

You are altogether beautiful,
my darling; there is no flaw in you.
Song of Songs 4:7 niv

• •

Some women pay a lot of money to have flawless skin. They use expensive beauty products, pay top dollar for cosmetologists, and have regular facials. They don't want a freckle or a pimple on their flawless faces.

Let's face it—most of us don't have flawless skin. Just the opposite, in fact. And the same is true with our bodies. We're always looking in the mirror and groaning at what we see.

How crazy that God says, "You are altogether beautiful, my darling," when He looks at you. He doesn't see the pimples. He doesn't see the cellulite or the chubby thighs. When He sees you, it's through eyes of love.

And check this out: He calls you flawless! "There is no flaw in you."

Whoa. You feel sure that's not true! You're riddled with flaws and imperfections, after all. So, why would God say this?

When He looks at you, His beautiful daughter, He sees you through the veil of what His Son, Jesus, did on the cross. Now that you're a child of the King, you really are flawless in His sight!

Wow, God! You see me as flawless because I put my trust in Jesus?
That's so amazing! I don't have to be perfect. You think I'm special
no matter what I look like. I'm so glad to hear this! Amen.

YOU CAN SOAR!

But those who hope in the LORD will renew their strength.
They will soar on wings like eagles; they will run and
not grow weary, they will walk and not be faint.
ISAIAH 40:31 NIV

You were born to fly, girl! No, really! According to today's verse, you can soar on wings like eagles when you put your hope in God. In other words, He will lift you above your circumstances and give you a whole new (heavenly) perspective.

When you realize that God is the one in charge, that you don't have to do everything on your own, you can rest easy. Do you feel the weight being lifted off your shoulders as you give your troubles to Him? Can you see the energy returning to your body once you realize it's not all on you?

You can run! You can soar! You can go above and beyond, doing more than you imagined, and all because you're doing it in God's power instead of your own.

Look around you at the people you know. Most of them are probably trying to make it on their own. They're like turkeys—grounded. They don't realize they were born to fly!

Someone must tell them. How about you?

I'm so grateful for the reminder that I don't have to carry
it all, Jesus. When I put my hope in You, I can soar. Amen.

CHILD OF DESTINY

"For I know the plans I have for you, declares the Lord,
plans for welfare and not for evil, to give you a future and a hope."
JEREMIAH 29:11 ESV

Queen Esther was a woman of destiny. When people talk about her, they say, "Oh, right! She's the one who was destined to save her people."

To be destined means it's ordained. It's meant to happen. You have a destiny too! There are places you'll go, things you'll do, that are meant only for you.

When you know you have a destiny, you're not scared of today—or tomorrow, for that matter. Girls with a destiny have their eyes on the prize.

When you understand you have a destiny, you can say the following statements and mean them with your whole heart:

> *I was born for a reason.*
> *I am not an accident.*
> *I have great things to do.*
> *God's power lives inside me.*
> *I'm destined to change the atmosphere around me.*

It's all true because you are a child of destiny!

It's so cool to think that I have a destiny, Lord.
You have big plans for me that I haven't even seen yet.
I will trust You as I move forward fearlessly into those
plans. I want to do great things for You. Amen.

A LOVELY CAKE

*And we know that for those who love God all
things work together for good, for those who
are called according to his purpose.*
ROMANS 8:28 ESV

Imagine you set out to bake a cake but left out the baking powder. That cake would fall flat! What if you left out the sugar? Ick. It might look okay, but looks can be deceiving. Now imagine you left out the liquid. What would happen?

Here's the point: some things are meant to work together.

Trusting in God is kind of like trusting in a cake before it's baked. You have to believe that all those ingredients will somehow work together and form something beautiful.

You've been through a lot in your young life, no doubt. And some of it has felt pretty impossible. But God. . .

He has somehow blended the good and the bad together in a lovely recipe, producing your beautiful life. You're the most exquisite cake, girl. Just go on trusting God with the process, and you'll do fine.

*There have been things in my life that haven't made sense, Jesus.
I haven't always understood. But I will go on trusting You no matter
what, because I know You're blending everything together into a
lovely story! Thank You for working things out, every time. Amen.*

GOD'S PURPOSE PREVAILS

"I make known the end from the beginning,
from ancient times, what is still to come. I say,
'My purpose will stand, and I will do all that I please.'"
ISAIAH 46:10 NIV

A scarlet thread has run all throughout the very long stretch of time from creation until now, showing us God's love for humanity. Even in the roughest of times, God's slender thread of hope has remained alive as His plans have advanced.

Isn't it cool to think that He has known everything that would ever happen even before it did? He saw it all, good and bad. And He's been there through it all, hard and easy.

God's purpose always prevails. Sin doesn't win. The enemy doesn't end up on top. We know how God's story comes to its conclusion. The Bible is clear that God, the ultimate winner, has a much bigger and deeper purpose than we could possibly understand.

Many things are stirring in this generation, and He has placed you squarely in the middle of it. Why? So that you could play a role in this season of history. Yes. . .you.

When I look back over the history of humankind, I sometimes
wonder how we got here, Jesus! There have been some
strange times, for sure! And there still are. But I trust You.
I place my hope and my destiny in Your hands, knowing
You're working everything together for Your good. Amen.

IF ONLY THEY HAD KNOWN

The wisdom I proclaim is God's secret wisdom, which is hidden from human beings, but which he had already chosen for our glory even before the world was made. None of the rulers of this world knew this wisdom. If they had known it, they would not have crucified the Lord of glory.

1 Corinthians 2:7–8 gnt

Did you ever wonder if the people who crucified Jesus ever realized what they'd done? Did they come to understand that they had taken the life of God in flesh? If so, how did they feel? Did any of them turn to God for forgiveness?

We don't always see the mistakes we're making as we're making them, but God is gracious and kind. He offers forgiveness even when we don't deserve it. (And let's face it: Do we ever deserve it?)

The sacrifice of Jesus on the cross was cloaked in love—for you and for every other human being who will call on the name of Jesus. He wants everyone to come to know Him no matter what mistakes they've made in the past.

So, today, as you face those not-so-great people who drive you crazy, do your best to offer grace in the same way Christ has offered it to you.

If only I had recognized the mistakes I was making before I made them, Jesus, I would have done things differently. Thank You for forgiving me and giving me wisdom and direction. Amen.

YOUR PERSONAL SCANNER

But it was to us that God made known his secret by
means of his Spirit. The Spirit searches everything,
even the hidden depths of God's purposes.
1 CORINTHIANS 2:10 GNT

- -

If you ever had a virus on your computer, you probably had to invest in a virus scanner. Basically, a scanner goes through every single file on your laptop or PC to look for bugs. When those bugs are found, they are eliminated so that the computer can run beautifully again.

You have your own personal built-in scanner, girl! The Holy Spirit lives inside of you, and He's on the move even now, rooting out anything that won't benefit you—spiritually, emotionally, or physically.

What does the Spirit find when He searches the deepest parts of you? Is there pain from something someone did to you years ago? Is there unforgiveness in your heart toward someone who took advantage of you? Are you still living with regrets over past decisions?

All those things belong in the trash! Today, give your heavenly Father permission to root out the things that are slowing you down so that you're free to run. That's what He wants for you, total freedom!

I'm sorry for letting things get stuck, Lord!
Today I give You permission to do a deep work.
Root out the things that no longer benefit me. Amen.

THE MIND OF GOD

As the scripture says, "Who knows the mind
of the Lord? Who is able to give him advice?"
We, however, have the mind of Christ.
1 Corinthians 2:16 gnt

• •

Have you ever wished you could read God's mind? Maybe you walked through a tough situation and got mad at Him because things weren't going the way you thought they would. Why? You prayed and prayed. Why wasn't He answering your prayers the way you wanted Him to?

Here's the truth, girl: If you could see inside the mind of God, you would be so overwhelmed! He's taking care of billions of people and everything else on the planet, but He still sees you. He still hears you. He still loves you even though He still has so many other things to take care of. In fact, He not only sees you but He also knows what's coming next. So perhaps that unanswered prayer is a protection to keep you from harm's way.

It takes courage to trust in God even when things aren't going your way. Esther understood this too. But she never gave up even when it looked like her whole world would fall apart. She kept going, and you can too.

I'm glad I can't see into Your mind, Jesus! I can't even
imagine how You keep up with it all. Thank You for
still loving me and keeping me on a safe road. Amen.

DIFFERENT MESSAGES

*We do, however, speak a message of wisdom among the mature,
but not the wisdom of this age or of the rulers of this age, who are
coming to nothing. No, we declare God's wisdom, a mystery that has
been hidden and that God destined for our glory before time began.*
1 Corinthians 2:6–7 niv

. . . .

Stop and listen to what is going on around you right now. Do you hear music playing? Dogs barking? People talking? TV shows blaring? Buzzers going off on the stove or the house alarm shrieking?

Life is noisy. Cars whiz by, horns honk, dogs yap, TVs blare, phones beep—and we can get inundated and overwhelmed by it all.

All those different noises are sending individual messages. The house alarm is crying, "Get out now!" The phone is beeping, "Answer the text from Mom!" The TV is saying, "Watch this great new series!" The dog is saying, "Someone's at the door!"

Some voices are harder to distinguish. A friend who's crying. A sibling who's yelling. You're not sure why they're so worked up. Discerning the problem takes effort.

There is a voice that you should strain to hear above all others, and that's the voice of the Spirit of God. He can offer wisdom to help you discern all those other blaring voices.

*I want to hear You above all the noise, God. I'll lean in close and
listen even when it's so noisy I can't hear myself think! Amen.*

SPIRIT-INFUSED WORDS

This is what we speak, not in words taught us by human wisdom but in words taught by the Spirit, explaining spiritual realities with Spirit-taught words.
1 Corinthians 2:13 niv

Have you ever said anything so profound, so helpful, that you wondered where the words came from? Maybe a friend came to you with a big problem, one she felt trapped by. You listened carefully to what she had to say, took a deep breath, and then shared a deep truth.

Oh, that truth didn't come from you. You didn't cook it up in your imagination. It was the Spirit of God speaking it to your heart. You just transferred it from your heart to your lips, and that truth changed everything for your friend.

If you listen closely, the Spirit is speaking. So if you're feeling overwhelmed or scared, listen for those "Spirit-taught" words, not your own. You probably have all sorts of ideas running through your mind on how to fix the situations you get yourself into, but those are like Band-Aids, temporary fixes. A true and lasting fix is Spirit infused and Spirit empowered.

Speak God's words, not yours. You never know whose world you might change. (It might even be your own!)

Holy Spirit, I will speak Your words over my situation. I won't put my little bandages on gaping wounds anymore. Amen.

BE TEACHABLE

*Do not deceive yourselves. If any of you think you
are wise by the standards of this age, you should
become "fools" so that you may become wise.*
1 Corinthians 3:18 niv

. . . .

Have you ever met a know-it-all? Know-it-alls are tough to be around. Some people would call them "unteachable." Oh, you can try, but no matter what you share with them, they always seem to know better, and they can't wait to tell you so.

Pride goes before a fall (Proverbs 16:18), but most of these folks don't know they're about to take a tumble. Instead, they go around with their noses in the air, making others feel stupid.

Don't be like that. Don't be a know-it-all. Even if you're the smartest girl in the room, you have plenty of room for growth. And this is one of the coolest things about following the Holy Spirit. He's right there to offer you wisdom well beyond your years (and certainly beyond anything you've ever learned in a classroom).

Be teachable. Be gentle. Be gracious. There's a huge difference between being smart and being wise. You want to be as wise as you can possibly be to navigate this complicated life.

*I get it, Jesus. It's okay to be book smart, but it's even better to
have the kind of wisdom that comes only from walking with
You. Help me become more like You—wise and loving. Amen.*

THE PERFECT LAWYER

My little children, I am writing these things to you so that you may not sin. But if anyone does sin, we have an advocate with the Father, Jesus Christ the righteous.

1 JOHN 2:1 ESV

If your mother got in a car accident but it wasn't her fault, the other person's insurance would have to pay up. Sometimes, though, the other person doesn't play nice. He lies to his insurance company and claims your mom was to blame. What do you do then?

Your mom would tell her side of the story, and if the insurance company still didn't believe her, she would probably end up hiring a lawyer. The lawyer would sue the insurance company for lots of money—maybe hundreds of thousands of dollars!

In this situation, the lawyer would serve as an advocate to represent your mom's side to the other person's insurance company. An advocate is the one who does the hard work of pleading your case so that you don't have to.

Jesus is your advocate. He's the one who stands in front of God, His Father, and says, "I have this one covered. She gave her heart to Me, and I'm taking her place."

You didn't have to do a thing. Your advocate took care of everything for you. What an amazing Savior He is!

Thank You for being my advocate, Jesus. You took care of absolutely everything, and I'm so grateful. Amen.

WE TRIUMPH BECAUSE OF LOVE

You give us great victories; in your
love you make us triumphant.
PSALM 89:17 GNT

. . . .

If you've ever watched a romance movie, you might have heard the hero (or heroine) say something like this: "Your love makes me a better person!"

It's true. When you feel deeply loved by someone else, you feel almost invincible. Their love causes you to triumph.

The same is true, but on a much grander scale, when we begin to recognize the love that God has for us. We can bask in that love and watch it transform and deliver us. And, just like that hero in the story, we see triumph after triumph as we rest in God's love.

We serve a victorious God. He's not coddling us to leave us in the cradle. He wants us to be mighty warriors for Him, to do great and culture-changing acts. Once you begin to recognize God's deep love for you, and for all of humankind, you want to do everything you can to make sure others experience this amazing love too.

Be emboldened by God's love today, daughter of God! Like Queen Esther in the throne room, rush to the King, and watch as His love transforms you, causing you to triumph!

I sense Your love, and it energizes me, Jesus! With Your love
embracing me, I feel invincible! Thank You for pouring
it out on me even when I don't deserve it. Amen.

A HEART TRANSPLANT

*"I will give you a new heart and put a new spirit in you;
I will remove from you your heart of stone and give you a
heart of flesh. And I will put my Spirit in you and move you
to follow my decrees and be careful to keep my laws."*
EZEKIEL 36:26–27 NIV

Have you ever known anyone who has had a heart transplant? Perhaps a little girl who was born with a weak heart. Or maybe an elderly man whose sick heart gave out on him. With modern technology, doctors can take the heart from a person who has recently passed away and put it into the chest of a very sick person, offering a new chance at life.

That's basically what Jesus did for you when He gave His life on the cross. He took your heart, riddled with sin, and swapped it out for His. What you're carrying around inside of you right now is the work of the greatest doctor of all time—God Almighty.

The heart transplant He offered you came with the promise of healthy living and eternal life. No earthly doctor can offer that! They can extend a life, but certainly not for eternity!

You might not always feel that new heart beating in your chest. There will be days when you're scared or lonely. But close your eyes and think about the heart transplant you've been through. With Jesus' heart beating inside you, you can do anything, girl!

*Thank You for my heart transplant, Jesus. I was withering
away until You came along. I'm so grateful. Amen.*

FULL OF HIS SPIRIT

"And in the last days it shall be, God declares, that I will pour out my Spirit on all flesh, and your sons and your daughters shall prophesy, and your young men shall see visions, and your old men shall dream dreams."

ACTS 2:17 ESV

In the book of Acts, you can read about the day the Holy Spirit fell on the disciples while they were praying in the upper room. Remarkable things happened! Tongues of fire came down, people spoke in other tongues (languages), and the disciples were filled with power and boldness, which they used to tell others the good news.

In these last days, the Spirit of God is moving in the earth. He's stirring believers to deeper faith, stronger vision, and courage to face the challenging times they're living in. Don't think that because you're living in an ungodly culture you can't make a difference. With the Spirit of God on your side, you can be just as powerful as the disciples were on that day in the upper room when the Spirit fell.

Today, ask God to pour out His Spirit on you. Every day, ask for an infilling, just like you would fill a car with gasoline. Don't rest until you've cried out, "God, fill me up!"

He will, you know. And once you're full, you will change the world!

Fill me up, Jesus! I want to be full of Your Spirit, just like the disciples were on the day of Pentecost. I don't want to be afraid of the culture around me. I want to impact it in a mighty way! Amen.

FORGIVENESS IS THE KEY

"For if you forgive other people when they sin against you,
your heavenly Father will also forgive you. But if you do not
forgive others their sins, your Father will not forgive your sins."
MATTHEW 6:14–15 NIV

Are you wondering why your trials haven't yet become triumphs? Maybe there's something in the way.

As you read today's verses, ponder the question "Is there anyone I need to forgive?"

It might seem like an odd question, but sometimes the reason we get stuck is that we're caught up in the hurts and pains of yesterday. We don't realize we've been holding someone in unforgiveness until the Holy Spirit whispers in our ear, "You know who you need to forgive."

Unforgiveness is like drinking bitter water. Swallow enough of it and you'll get sick. It takes courage to admit to God that you've been hanging on to unforgiveness, but He already knows it anyway.

Choose today to forgive so that you can be forgiven. And if there's anyone you've hurt who might need to forgive you, make it easy on them. Go to that person and say these twelve life-changing words: "I am sorry. I was wrong. Please forgive me. I love you." Those twelve words can heal almost any relationship if said with love, grace, and sincerity. Yes, it will take courage. Yes, it will be worth it.

Show me how to forgive those who have hurt me, Jesus. Amen.

YOUR TENDER SHEPHERD

*Know that the Lord, he is God! It is he who made us, and we
are his; we are his people, and the sheep of his pasture.*
PSALM 100:3 ESV

Picture a tiny baby sheep, born way too soon. The shepherd doesn't
think she's going to make it, so he takes extra care to keep her warm
and make sure she has plenty of milk.

Thanks to his tender loving care (and the love of the mama sheep),
the baby pulls through. Before long, she's full grown and strong, running
in the field alongside all the others.

The shepherd has a special place in his heart for that one because
he rescued her from nearly dying. So he gives her a lot of love and attention all her life.

In some ways, you're like that little sheep. You've been down in the
pit. There were days when you wondered if you would make it. You've
been through personal tragedies and hard times. But God, the tender
Shepherd, picked you up and turned those tragedies into triumphs.

Why does He care so much for you? Because you're His own child.
As today's verse says, you're "the sheep of his pasture."

Your Good Shepherd will always have a special place in His heart
for you. Doesn't that give you a real boost? He'll never let you down!

*Lord, knowing that I'm safe in Your flock gives me
courage to face whatever comes my way. Amen.*

HE WILL FIGHT FOR YOU

*"For the LORD your God is he who goes with you to fight
for you against your enemies, to give you the victory."*
DEUTERONOMY 20:4 ESV

Even the best warrior, fully suited up, is defenseless unless the Lord goes with him. This life you're facing is a battle. You've probably had days when you came home from school feeling bloody and bruised. Life is hard.

But God goes with you. This should embolden you, knowing He's in the battle alongside you. So arm up. Suit up. Do all you can do to be prepared. But more than anything else, stick close to God. Ask Him to guide you, to help you. He will, you know. You're His adored child.

You'll face enemies ahead. That's inevitable. But knowing that God is with you should bring great peace. He will give you victory. Don't give up!

*I'm so battle weary, Jesus! I don't feel like fighting anymore.
Seems all I do is lose anyway. Thank You for the reminder that I
don't have to lose, because You're on my side. You're right there,
in the thick of the battle, alongside me. Thank You for giving me
the victory over every situation, even the hardest ones. Amen.*

HE'S ON YOUR SIDE

With God on our side we will win; he will defeat our enemies.
PSALM 108:13 GNT

Have you ever walked away from a tough situation, one where you embarrassed yourself with something you said or did, and muttered, "Well, that was dumb!"

The truth is we often do or say stupid things. It's inevitable. We're human, after all. This can be particularly humiliating in the heat of a battle when you end up looking like a goober and the other person ends up feeling victorious over you.

Even in those inevitable moments, however, God won't let you down. You might feel squashed right now. You might even be humiliated. But there's coming a day when God will vindicate you. With Him on your side, you will win.

Okay, winning doesn't always look like you think it will. You won't sit on a throne and reign over the other kids who annoy you. It might look more like a peace pact between you and that girl who has always irritated you. Or maybe it will look like friends finally coming together and getting along after a long season of being angry with each other.

No matter what battles you're facing, they won't all end in failure as you have feared. God hasn't forgotten you. He's fighting for you even now.

Lord, how many times have I done or said something
embarrassing in front of those who treat me as
their enemy? Help me overcome. Amen.

YOU WERE BORN TO OVERCOME

For everyone who has been born of God overcomes the world.
And this is the victory that has overcome the world—our faith.
1 JOHN 5:4 ESV

Did you know that you've been born twice? It's true. The first time, your mom gave birth to you. The second time, you were born of the Spirit when you gave your heart to Christ. (You've done that, right?)

Now look at this verse in light of all that. It says that everyone who has been born of God (your second birth) overcomes the world.

Whoa. It doesn't always feel like it, of course. There are things in this world that seem to be overcoming you, no doubt, not the other way around. But in the end, you will overcome. You'll overcome temptations if you place your trust in Christ. You'll overcome your anger and bitterness if you offer forgiveness. You'll overcome relational issues if you give them to God to heal.

There's really nothing in this life that can hold you back. You can have the same kind of victory that army captains have! You can march boldly, proudly, and courageously because you've overcome in so many different areas of your life.

Don't ever think you're a failure. You're not. You're a victor, girl. Live it!

I'm born of the Spirit, and I'm victorious in You,
Jesus! Thank You for that reminder! Amen.

THE FINISH LINE

For though the righteous fall seven times, they rise again,
but the wicked stumble when calamity strikes.
PROVERBS 24:16 NIV

Have you ever watched a video of a marathon runner dragging toward the finish line? Maybe he's fallen multiple times. But there he is, about to finish the race like the others. He looks terrible. You wonder if he'll be all right. But he crosses that line, even in his condition.

The Bible says that your faith walk is a bit like that. You've been running a really long race. It took courage just to sign up for it! But here you are, running along—and you're tired. You've fallen more times than you can count, and you're weary. You see the finish line up ahead, but you wonder if you're going to make it.

Be encouraged! Today's verse gives you a clear answer. You will make it! You'll cross that finish line victorious! There will be others in the race who will fall by the wayside. They won't get up again. They won't cross that line. But you, daughter of God? You're destined to triumph, to win the race!

Don't give up when you've made so much progress already. Even if you're in a tough period right now, it will pass. You will be victorious. Keep running, girl.

I won't give up! I can see the finish line in sight,
Jesus. Thank You for making me victorious! Amen.

A TRIUMPHANT PARADE

But thanks be to God, who always leads us as captives
in Christ's triumphal procession and uses us to spread
the aroma of the knowledge of him everywhere.
2 Corinthians 2:14 niv

Have you ever been caught up in a parade? Maybe you found yourself marching alongside the performers as they made their way up the street, drums playing, majorettes twirling, and folks cheering from the sidelines.

Your relationship with Jesus is kind of like being in a parade. He moves you forward, along with millions of other believers, in triumphal procession.

There's a huge difference between a parade and a funeral. In a parade, everyone is smiling as they move forward. But in a funeral procession, everyone is somber and crying as they make their way to the graveside.

Make sure your life is more like a parade than a funeral march. You have so much to be grateful for, so much to celebrate. Christ is at the front of the line, cheering you on, encouraging you to see that the outcome of this parade will be heavenly. Literally.

I don't always see the glass as half-full, Jesus.
Sometimes my life is more like a funeral procession.
Help me to keep the right perspective and to be
courageous as I march, march, march along! Amen.

WHO CAN STAND AGAINST US?

What then shall we say to these things?
If God is for us, who can be against us?
ROMANS 8:31 ESV

. . . .

No doubt Queen Esther was scared as she entered the throne room without an invitation. But maybe not as afraid as you might think. After all, she had the God of creation on her side—and she knew it. When God is on your side, who can possibly prevail against you?

Don't believe it? Read the story of David and Goliath. That vicious Philistine giant couldn't take down the little shepherd boy.

Read the story of Joshua and the battle of Jericho. God caused the walls of the city to collapse!

Read the story of Paul and Silas in prison. They began to sing songs of praise, and an earthquake shook the prison and busted their chains, setting them free!

God can do whatever He wants whenever He wants. So don't be afraid, no matter what you're walking through. The same God who delivered Esther, David, Joshua, Paul, and Silas will deliver you! Your chains will be broken, your enemies will fall, your people will be rescued, and you will live in safety.

Why? Because you're a daughter of the King, of course!

I want to have the faith of Esther, David, and the others,
Lord! Thank You for the reminder that You are God and You
can rescue me no matter what I'm going through. Amen.

THE THINGS WE CANNOT SEE

To have faith is to be sure of the things we hope for,
to be certain of the things we cannot see.
HEBREWS 11:1 GNT

When you flip the switch on the wall, you have faith that the lights will come on. When you hit the ignition of the car, you have faith that the car will start. When you twist the knobs next to the faucet, you have faith that water will come pouring out.

You're sure of a lot of things even before they happen. Before the lights come on. Before the car starts. Before the water flows. Even before all of that, you're sure it will happen. You have no doubt, in fact.

You can be just as sure of God coming through for you. He's baking up amazing plans even now. He's flipping switches in hard situations. He's causing change even when you can't see it.

You can trust God with the things you can't yet see. Those miracles you're waiting for? Don't give up. Just keep trusting.

I can't see the outcome yet, Jesus, but You can, and I know I
can trust You. You are even more trustworthy than the light
switch, the car key, and the faucet. You are all-powerful,
and You love me, so I will place my trust in You. Amen.

PRAISE YOUR WAY THROUGH

Is anyone among you suffering? Let him pray.
Is anyone cheerful? Let him sing praise.
JAMES 5:13 ESV

. . . .

God didn't promise that hard times won't come. There's nothing in the Bible that says, "Hey, if you're a Christian, you're immune to trouble." On the contrary, the Bible confirms that troubles will come, but God will go through them with you.

When you're in the middle of a true battle, there's one weapon (a tool) that can help you power through. Praise. It might not make much sense, but if you begin to praise God even when you don't feel like it, even when the enemy is hard on your heels, you will be energized in a way you didn't even expect.

Praise is an activator, like baking powder in a cake. When you add it to the mix, things take off in a big way.

So activate your faith with praise today. Sing a worship song. Write one of your own if you want to. Lift your heart and your voice in praise to God even when it doesn't make sense, and then watch Him move!

I will lift my voice in praise even when I don't feel like it, Lord!
If I'm going through it, I won't be stopped from praising You. Amen.

HIS PEACE IS GREATER

The peace of God, which surpasses all understanding,
will guard your hearts and your minds in Christ Jesus.
PHILIPPIANS 4:7 ESV

When you think of the word *peace*, what image comes to mind? Maybe you see a cozy blanket, one you can wrap yourself up in on a chilly day. Perhaps you think of a roaring fire in the fireplace. Maybe "peace" comes when you fall into bed at the end of a long day and finally put your head on the pillow.

Here's the thing: God's peace is greater than anything you're facing. It's cozier than that blanket, more comforting than a warm fire, and even better than resting your head on a pillow.

You can have God's peace, right in the middle of the storm. Today, as you're facing challenge after challenge, don't let your heart be anxious. Instead, take a deep breath and remind yourself, "God's peace is greater. I have nothing to be afraid of."

And remember, the best way to have peace during the chaos is to ask. God is right there, waiting for you to crawl in His lap and ask. So spend time with Him and watch those troubles fade away.

Your peace is greater, Lord. Greater than the teacher who seems to dislike me. Greater than the so-called friends who talk behind my back. Greater than my feelings. I'm so grateful that I can have Your peace no matter what I'm going through. Amen.

LEAVE A LEGACY

*That the next generation might know them, the children
yet unborn, and arise and tell them to their children.*
PSALM 78:6 ESV

When you think of the word *legacy*, what comes to mind? Do you think of grandmothers and grandfathers passing down family heirlooms? Are you reminded of a house that your grandparents once lived in that now belongs to an aunt or uncle?

A legacy can include those things, of course, but the greatest legacy someone can pass down to the next generation is a good foundation in the Word of God. There's something to be said for a praying mother or grandmother. It's priceless to have a dad or uncle or grandpa who believes in Jesus and takes his family to church.

One day it will be your turn. You can keep this courageous gospel legacy going with future generations. Staying strong in your faith will ensure that your children one day hear about the Lord. (And with things going the way they are in the world, you can't count on anyone else to tell them!)

Be a legacy leaver. Establish in your heart and mind right here, right now, that future generations of your family will know and love Jesus as you do. How wonderful to have a faith that spans multiple generations!

*I am so grateful for my relationship with You, Jesus. I want
everyone to have that. Help me remain strong so that
the legacy can continue for years to come. Amen.*

YOUR LIFE'S IMPRINT

Let this be recorded for a generation to come, so that
a people yet to be created may praise the L ORD.
P SALM 102:18 ESV

Imagine you stumbled across your grandmother's diary from when she was a little girl. You would likely read every word, trying to imagine how she felt, what she looked like, and whether you were like her.

Knowing where you've come from helps with knowing where you're going. It's good to have some record of our previous generations so we can keep the family heritage going, after all.

In the twenty-first century, it's easy to document things. You can take pictures, film videos, and write down all your innermost thoughts on a blog or in a personal diary.

Why is it important to leave an imprint of your life? Because one day your grandchildren might be looking back, wondering what you were like! Let them know—through the words you pen—that you loved Jesus and you loved your family. Don't let all your personal writings be filled with teenage angst. Remember, there's coming a day when people might be reading all that!

I want to document my life, Jesus, to leave an
imprint on this world. Show me how I can do this—
for this current generation and for generations to come!
Help me spread the gospel in every way I can. Amen.

PASS IT ON

*"You shall love the L*ORD *your God with all your heart and with all your soul and with all your might. And these words that I command you today shall be on your heart. You shall teach them diligently to your children, and shall talk of them when you sit in your house, and when you walk by the way, and when you lie down, and when you rise."*

DEUTERONOMY 6:5–7 ESV

How do you keep the message of the gospel going, not just in your lifetime, but in generations to come? It's simple: tell the children.

Tell the children all the things you've learned in your walk with Jesus. If you don't have younger siblings, tell your nieces and nephews. Tell the kids in the neighborhood. Offer to teach kids at your church.

If you share the love of Christ with a child, that child isn't as likely to reject it. You can do it in a casual way. You don't have to pound them with Bible verses. Just share the things of God with kids in a natural, comfortable way. While you're eating. While you're playing.

You could be a catalyst for a young child to come to know the Lord. Think about that. A little girl who is feeling alone and afraid right now could be boosted with confidence by tomorrow if you would just take the time to tell her about your walk with Jesus. It's really that simple.

I won't hold back! I'll do what scripture says, Jesus. I'll pass down the legacy of faith, not just to children in my family, but to others I meet as well. Amen.

LET THE CHILDREN COME

"Let the children come to me, and do not stop them,
because the Kingdom of God belongs to such as these."
MARK 10:14 GNT

Jesus was teaching, and a group of children approached. His disciples, thinking they were doing Jesus a favor, tried to push the kids away. They didn't think Jesus would want to be bothered with a bunch of kids.

On the contrary! Jesus very much wanted the children to spend time with Him. So He chewed out the disciples and said, "Let them come. Don't hinder them." In other words, don't prevent them. They're just as important as the grown folks!

He went on to say something incredibly profound, something that probably shocked His disciples and the religious men in the crowd. Referring to the kids, Jesus said, "The Kingdom of God belongs to such as these."

Whoa. Was He really saying that those kids had a place waiting for them in heaven too? They weren't religious. They hadn't preached or shared the gospel. They were just kids, created in God's image!

Jesus was trying to convey the point that you have to have the faith of a child to enter heaven. Children are trusting and filled with faith. So treat kids the way Jesus would, and watch as they change the world.

I guess "Jesus Loves the Little Children" is more
than just a song. Right, Jesus? I'm guessing it
might be Your very favorite, in fact. Amen.

TELL THE STORIES

And he said to the people of Israel, "In the future, when your children ask you what these stones mean, you will tell them about the time when Israel crossed the Jordan on dry ground."
JOSHUA 4:21–22 GNT

· ·

Picture this: The Israelites had traveled from Egypt to the promised land. The journey took a lot longer than they expected, but they finally made it. As they reached the Jordan, a river usually full and teeming with life, God made a way for them to cross on dry land.

So that they would never forget, they left twelve stones in the water. Why? Well, today's scripture explains: "In the future, when your children ask you what these stones mean, you will tell them about the time when Israel crossed the Jordan on dry ground."

The stones were meant to be a physical testimony to the miracle God had worked on their behalf. He wanted the story of that miracle to be passed down from generation to generation.

No doubt there are miraculous stories in your family too. Keep 'em going, girl! Share them with the kids. Share them with your relatives. Make sure everyone knows about that time God healed your aunt Cindy or that time your father lost his job but found an even better one.

Confidence is boosted with testimonies. Courage is boosted with testimonies. And people will come to know Christ because of the word of your testimony. So don't be scared. Speak up!

I will share the stories of what You've done, Jesus! Amen.

LET'S TALK ABOUT GRANDPARENTS

Grandchildren are the crowning glory of the aged;
parents are the pride of their children.
PROVERBS 17:6 NLT

. . . .

There's much to be said for the bond of a loving family. When you're surrounded by people who love you, you feel like you can conquer the world.

Look at today's verse. Let's pause to talk about grandparents for a moment. Did you realize that you, the grandchild, are the crowning glory of your grandparents? What do you suppose that means? And how does that make you feel?

You are your grandmother's legacy. You are your grandfather's legacy. They're so proud of you, they could bust their buttons. And for those who are blessed enough to have godly grandparents, consider this: It was probably their prayers that led your parents to have a life of faith. And it might have been your grandparents' prayers that led you to the Lord too.

Family is a part of God's amazing plan. So stick close and love them even on difficult days. One day a little girl might just look at you—her grandmother—and say, "Grandma, what was life like when you were a kid?"

I'm part of a long line of people who are all linked
together as one big family. . .and I'm so grateful, Jesus.
Thank You for the legacy that was passed to me. Amen.

MAKE A NEW PATH

*"Choose this day whom you will serve, whether the gods
your fathers served in the region beyond the River,
or the gods of the Amorites in whose land you dwell.
But as for me and my house, we will serve the Lord."*
JOSHUA 24:15 ESV

Maybe you didn't come from a lineage of faith. Maybe you're the first person in your family to come to know Christ. What a wonderful opportunity to share the good news with others!

Okay, so it might not be easy. Those who don't know Him might not understand your new zeal for Jesus or those Bible verses you've been quoting.

In some ways, people in that position are a lot like the Israelites who left Egypt. Some of them had given themselves over to pagan ways and started living a life contrary to the things of the Lord. God asked them to make a choice: "Choose today who you're going to serve. It's going to be either the false gods of your fathers or the one true God."

God is saying the same thing today. Even if your parents, grandparents, and so on aren't Christians, you can still blaze a new path. You can still leave a legacy for those who come behind you. You can courageously move forward with a testimony that will change future generations of your family. Wow! What an amazing privilege!

*Show me the path, and I'll walk in it, Jesus! I want to
leave a legacy for those who come behind me. Amen.*

HE LOVED, HE GAVE

"For God so loved the world, that he gave his only Son, that whoever believes in him should not perish but have eternal life."
JOHN 3:16 ESV

Because God loved, He gave. And that's exactly what He wants you to do too.

It's not always easy in today's culture to be a giver, but when you pour out your life on behalf of others, you're living like Jesus.

And isn't that the point of all this? He healed the sick, fed the hungry, and gave His life for humankind in a gruesome death on the cross. No matter what life required of Him, He gave it—and more.

When you live like that, you get bolder every single day. The more you give, the stronger you become. The braver you become.

That's how Esther lived. She was just a simple girl, never dreaming of the lives she would impact. But because she loved her people, she gave—and look at how that turned out!

Give yourself away like she did. Then watch as the Spirit of God infuses you with a holy, invigorating power that surprises everyone, even you!

I will give myself away, Lord. You loved, and You gave. I love people too. I don't always show it, but I do. Teach me how to live for others, as You did, so that I can live a courageous lifestyle. Amen.

SCRIPTURE INDEX

OLD TESTAMENT

NEW TESTAMENT

MORE ENCOURAGEMENT FOR YOUR BEAUTIFUL SPIRIT!

YOU BELONG
Devotions and Prayers for a Teen Girl's Heart

**You Were Created with Purpose by a
Loving, Heavenly Creator. . .You Belong!**

This delightful devotional is a lovely reminder that you were created with purpose by a heavenly Creator. . .and that you belong— right here and now—in this world. 180 encouraging readings and inspiring prayers, rooted in biblical truth, will reassure your uncertain heart, helping you to understand that you're *never* alone and *always* loved. In each devotional reading, you will encounter the bountiful blessings and grace of your Creator, while coming to trust His purposeful plan for you in this world.

Flexible Casebound / 978-1-63609-169-3